THE
SPIRIT
CALLING

Resting in the Quiet
of the Still, Small Voice

WORTHY
PUBLISHING

Library of Congress Control Number: 2012913515

Produced with the assistance of Livingstone, the Publishing Services Division of eChristian, Inc. Project staff includes: Linda Taylor, Linda Washington, Carol Chaffee Fielding, Dave Veerman, Larry Taylor, Ashley Taylor, and Tom Shumaker.

For foreign and subsidiary rights, contact Riggins International Rights Services, Inc.; www.rigginsrights.com

ISBN: 978-1-61795-114-5 (hardcover)

Cover and interior design: Christopher Tobias, Tobias Design
Cover photography: ©Evelina Kremsdork/archangel images; ©Keith Webber Jr./istockphoto
Interior photography: Fotolia

Printed in the United States of America

12 13 14 15 16 17   LBM   8 7 6 5 4 3 2 1

WELCOME

Before Jesus was crucified, arose from the grave, and returned to heaven, he well understood that those he would leave behind needed special power and encouragement in order to carry out the tasks he had given them. He warned them of coming persecution, but then sought to reassure his followers:

> These things I have spoken to you while being present with you. But the Helper, the Holy Spirit, whom the Father will send in My name, He will teach you all things, and bring to your remembrance all things that I said to you. Peace I leave with you, My peace I give to you; not as the world gives do I give to you. Let not your heart be troubled, neither let it be afraid. (John 14:25–27 NKJV)

Clearly, the Spirit is an ever-present helper (other translations say "counselor" or "advocate") sent to teach us, to remind us, and to bring us peace in a world that is all too often *not* peaceful. The presence of the Holy Spirit empowers every believer for the task of growing closer to Christ and growing his kingdom here on earth.

We have created this book to help you get to know the Spirit better and to learn more about the fruit he is cultivating in you. For the first three months you will read about the promise, the character, and the work of the Holy Spirit. Then you will have the opportunity to focus on each fruit of the Spirit—love, joy, peace, patience, kindness, goodness, faithfulness, gentleness, and self-control—one month at a time. The daily readings include a key verse from Scripture, a brief devotional written as though the Spirit is speaking to you, a lengthier reading from Scripture, and a short prayer starter.

We pray that as you read *The Spirit Calling*, you truly will be able to rest in the quiet of his still, small voice. May this be a year of great harvest in your life as you hear the Spirit calling.

—The Publisher

CONTRIBUTORS

Ashlee Amann

Greg Asimakoupoulos

Marija Birchard

Kyle Carruthers

Sarah Cespedes

Carolyn Cilento

Ryan Dennison

Carol Chaffee Fielding

Kacey Heinlein

Dennis Hensley

Katelyn Irons

David Jorgensen

Kathy Lay

Lexie Owen

Jeremy Paul

John Perrodin

Demelza Ramirez

Sue Rosenfeld

Betsy Schmitt

Elise Speiser

Joshua Spotts

Tom Vick

Linda Washington

JANUARY

THE PROMISE OF THE SPIRIT

JANUARY 1

Now the earth was formless and empty, darkness was over the surface of the deep, and the Spirit of God was hovering over the waters.

—**Genesis 1:2** (NIV)

I WAS THERE

I hovered over the depths, waiting. Nothing on earth existed at that point. It was dark and empty. But then the Father called all of creation into being. The formlessness, the emptiness, the darkness became form and fullness, filled with light.

You see, I have always been with God and the Son— the three of us in holy Trinity, holy unity. In those early moments before all of creation was spoken into being, I was there, present. Before anything else was, the Father, Son, and I existed. We have always been and always will be for all eternity.

You can count on that, dear one. The promises in Scripture are promises you know will come true. We who created something out of nothing can take your life and make it all it is meant to be. Start this year with that realization.

It will make all the difference.

Read Genesis 1.

Lord, in this new year, take me and use me to your glory.

JANUARY 2

As Jesus came up out of the water, the heavens were opened and he saw the Spirit of God descending like a dove and settling on him.

—**Matthew 3:16** (NLT)

YOU BRING JOY

The Son became flesh, born as a baby on Planet Earth. It was all in the plan from the beginning. The Father knew that his children would disappoint him, that they would fall into sin and need a Savior. He told the Satan-serpent that one day a Savior would come: "He will strike your head, and you will strike his heel" (Genesis 3:15 NLT). Satan would cause a wound, but the Son would deal the deathblow.

The day Jesus began his earthly ministry, I descended and settled upon him. The Father said, "This is my dearly loved Son, who brings me great joy" (Matthew 3:17 NLT).

Just as I was with the Son, I am with you. The Father sent me to draw close to you always. You are his beloved child, and you also bring him great joy.

Read Matthew 3:13–17.

Help me to bring you great joy today.

JANUARY 3

The Spirit is poured out upon us from on high, and the wilderness becomes a fertile field, and the fertile field is considered as a forest.

—Isaiah 32:15 (NASB)

LEAVING THE WILDERNESS BEHIND

Precious one, I know you walked through the wilderness. Your life felt dry, desolate, with no hope of relief in sight. But when you heard my call, a spring of hope bubbled in your heart.

You followed my lead as I drew you to the pool of living water. All of heaven rejoiced when you knelt, drank, were made clean, and were filled to overflowing. Your wilderness has become a fruitful field as you committed yourself to reading God's Word and following the example of Jesus. As you continue to learn about me and gradually turn more of your life over to me, the fruitful fields of your heart will become a mighty forest.

You have friends and family who wander in the wilderness. Share my fruit with them. Pray that they will be open to my leading just as you were.

Read Isaiah 32.

Thank you for leading me out of the wilderness and into a fruitful life.

For I will pour water on him who is thirsty, and floods on the dry ground; I will pour My Spirit on your descendants, and My blessing on your offspring.

—**Isaiah 44:3** (NKJV)

THE SPIRIT BRINGS BLESSINGS

God is a patient, loving Father and a God of justice. I am poured out on those who love God and withheld from those who hate the Lord.

When the children of Israel rebelled against me, I was withheld from the children and grandchildren of those who actively served other gods. This should be a frightening warning for everyone who loves his family!

Yet through the prophet Isaiah, the promise of a Messiah was given. Like a flood, I would be poured out upon the descendants of Jacob and others. The thirsty ground of their barren souls would receive streams of living water.

Child, do you thirst? Come to me and drink. Pass on the promise of my blessed indwelling to future generations.

Read Isaiah 44:1–8.

Help me to always hunger and thirst for you and to be an example to future generations.

JANUARY 5

I will not hide my face anymore from them, when I pour out my Spirit upon the house of Israel, declares the Lord GOD.

—**Ezekiel 39:29** (ESV)

I AM NOT HIDDEN FROM YOU

The prophet Isaiah proclaimed this truth: "Seek the LORD while he may be found; call upon him while he is near" (Isaiah 55:6 ESV).

Dear one, I am always near to you. I was sent into the world when Jesus ascended into heaven so you would not be left alone. I'm here to guide you, along with my holy Word. I'm here to comfort you when you feel as though you've been betrayed and abandoned. I'm here to intercede for you at the very throne of God when you just can't find the words to pray.

Because Jesus sacrificed himself for you, I cannot be hidden from you. Instead, I am poured out for you. I bring my fruit into your life that you may mature in your faith and grow to become more like Jesus.

Read Ezekiel 39:25–29.

Lord, thank you for sending your Holy Spirit so I don't have to travel this life alone.

JANUARY 6

*And it shall come to pass
afterward that I will pour out
My Spirit on all flesh; your
sons and your daughters shall
prophesy.*

—Joel 2:28 (NKJV)

NO LIMITATIONS

I am so glad you are alive in this epoch of history. Long ago my presence was limited to a few select kings and prophets. I would draw near to them and give them wisdom for the circumstances they faced. But because of Jesus, that has all changed now. There is no longer any limitation as to who may experience my presence or my power. The Father has given me permission to fill you and empower you just like I did David and Isaiah and Huldah.

It doesn't matter to me if you are young or old. I'm not concerned if you are male or female. My desire is to envelop you today so that you can accomplish God's purpose without fear or compromise. I will fill your heart with dreams and your mind with ideas that will help to extend the boundaries of God's kingdom. Trust me!

Read
Joel 2:28–29.

*I'm humbled I can be a
conduit for your purposes
in my world.*

JANUARY 7

By day the LORD went ahead of them in a pillar of cloud to guide them on their way and by night in a pillar of fire to give them light, so that they could travel by day or night.

—Exodus 13:21 (NIV)

24/7 PROVISION

While the Israelites trudged through the barren wilderness, they saw a cloud and they saw fire in the sky—the signs of my presence. I was their GPS, making sure they were heading in the right direction. I was also their traffic signal. When I moved, they knew they had a green light to proceed. When I stopped, this was their red light.

I also provided them with comfort day and night. During the blistering heat of the day, my cloud buffered them from direct exposure to the sun. During the cold nights, my fire provided them necessary warmth.

Precious one, I hope you understand that my nature is still the same. I long to guide you and to comfort you as you journey through your own personal wilderness. Will you let me?

Read Exodus 13:17–22.

Lord, I am grateful for your guidance.

JANUARY 8

Like cattle that go down to the
plain, they were given rest by
the Spirit of the LORD.

—**Isaiah 63:14** (NIV)

DESERT'S REST

I remember the desert that day, the searing heat rising
from the coarse, hot sand. How it surged into the
Israelites' feet, filling their minds with doubts of our love
for them. They turned against my touch; they rebelled and
cast aside the promises I provided through Moses. Yet I
still comforted them and gave them rest. I faithfully kept
my promise to give them a home.

Child, I can deliver the same kind of rest for your
weary soul. I see how you sometimes run to and fro,
seeking counsel and following plans other than mine. Your
efforts parch you and leave you depleted. Don't you know
how loved you are?

I will give you rest if you will trust me.

Read
Isaiah 63:7–19.

Lord, I need the peace
you promise to give.
My heart is waiting
for yours.

JANUARY 9

Then He replied, "My presence will go with you, and I will give you rest."

—**Exodus 33:14** (HCSB)

THE PROMISE OF REST

Child, are you weary today? Frazzled, confused, unsure what this day will bring or how you will get through it? Are you wondering which direction to go, what path to follow? Just as I led my chosen ones from slavery into freedom, from the desert into the Promised Land, I will lead you from your worries and anxious thoughts into rest. Even when Israel disappointed me and gave their love to man-made, worthless idols, I did not turn my face from them. When my servant and friend Moses came to me and asked for guidance, I gave him the assurance of my presence and rest. Will I not do the same for you?

Allow me to walk with you this day. Cast your burdens and your anxious thoughts on me. I will lead you in love and wisdom, and I will give you rest.

Read Exodus 33.

Fill me with your presence today. Quiet my anxious thoughts and usher me into your rest.

You sent your good Spirit to instruct them, and you did not stop giving them manna from heaven or water for their thirst.

—**Nehemiah 9:20** (NLT)

HEAVENLY INSTRUCTION

Venturing into the unknown can be daunting. It is difficult to leave the comfortable and familiar for the strange and new—even when your current situation may be unbearable. Consider the Hebrews. Although they were finally free from the bondage of Egyptian slavery, they nearly allowed fear of the future to turn them back to slavery! Then, as they returned to their homeland and sought to rebuild their city, not knowing what lay ahead, they needed to be reminded of my mercy and grace. Through it all, I sustained the people of Israel, not only giving them food and water but instructing them every step of the way. For forty years, they lacked nothing. Their feet never swelled; their clothing never wore out.

Where you are heading today, amid the unknowns you are facing, do not be afraid. I am there. If you will listen to my voice, I will instruct you and teach you. You will lack for nothing.

Read Nehemiah 9:17–21.

Spirit, I seek your instruction today. Teach me what I need to know to face the unknown.

JANUARY 11

And I will ask the Father, and he will give you another advocate to help you and be with you forever—the Spirit of truth.

—John 14:16–17 (NIV)

YOUR CHAMPION

Everyone needs a champion, someone to encourage them and cheer them on when life gets difficult. Jesus understood this. He knew what his disciples would face in the future. He knew what you would be facing too. That's why he promised his followers, then and now, an advocate—the Spirit of truth. As I did for the bewildered and discouraged disciples following the Crucifixion, the early church in the face of persecution, and for all of God's children through the ages, I am here to speak the truth, to inspire, and to remind you of the Father's love for you, expressed through the Son.

When others tear you down, I am there. When the world lies to you, I am there. When you are discouraged and downtrodden, I am there. I am your Champion, your Advocate, and your Cheerleader. Always.

Read
John 14:16–26.

Thank you, Spirit of truth, for being with me always and encouraging me. Be my advocate today.

JANUARY 12

*Do you not know that you are
God's temple and that God's
Spirit dwells in you?*

—1 Corinthians 3:16 (ESV)

GOD'S HOLY TEMPLE

When my people Israel wandered in the desert for forty years, I dwelled among them in a traveling tent, the tabernacle. Later, when my people were a nation, I instructed King Solomon to build a glorious temple, where my presence abided in the Holy of Holies. Only the high priest was permitted to enter, and only on prescribed occasions. The rituals and instructions were precise and to be obeyed or certain death would follow. All that changed with a babe born in a lowly manger, a torn curtain, and a broken body.

Today, you are the temple of God, and I dwell within you. I am with you upon your waking, in your sleep, in your health, and in the midst of sickness. I am with you in your struggles and in your victories. When you are at your loneliest, your most vulnerable, I am there. When you need wisdom, grace, forgiveness, or encouragement, I am there.

As you enter your day, no matter what you may encounter, I am with you.

**Read
1 Corinthians 3:16.**

*Indwelling Spirit, go
with me this day and
remind me throughout
my interactions that you
are with me always.*

Don't you realize that your body is the temple of the Holy Spirit, who lives in you and was given to you by God?
—**1 Corinthians 6:19** (NLT)

MY HOLY TEMPLE

When you received me, your sins were forgiven, and you were granted a place at the heavenly table. The Father cleansed your soul so I could dwell in you, guide your steps, and interpret your groans.

Beloved, although the Father has forgiven you and continues to forgive, do not be like the Corinthians and think, *I am allowed to do anything* (1 Corinthians 6:12 NLT).

You were united with the Son when I came to live in you. Therefore, do not take part in things that do not glorify him. Worldly indulgences have no value at the heavenly seat promised to you. Flee from sexual immorality.

I desire to fill the holes of your life with the Father's love, just as you desire for them to be filled. I beg you, remain pure. Keep my temple holy, and honor the Father with your body.

Read
1 Corinthians 6.

I commit my body to holiness and purity so it may be a temple for your Spirit.

He saved us through the washing of rebirth and renewal by the Holy Spirit.

—Titus 3:5 (NIV)

HE SAVED YOU

Child, I know your talents and your capacity for greatness. I have given you that capacity. Yet you know that you could not save yourself through any means. Only Jesus could save you.

Through faith in Jesus I offer you a new life, a new identity that is perfect and flawless in me. Come to me. I can renew you when you fall and carry the weight of your burdens. I promise to do this because I love you.

The Son washed the feet of his disciples and I will wash your heart, beloved child. I will renew you and fill you with myself so that you might be saved. My mercy is for you. My cleansing is for you.

Read Titus 3.

Wash me clean, O God, and renew a right spirit within me.

JANUARY 15

*The Lord God and His Spirit
have sent Me.*

—**Isaiah 48:16** (NKJV)

COUNT ON ME

You're lonely. You're hurting. You're tired and you're
wondering, *How can I be assured that I'm not alone?*
I am with you. From the beginning of time, I have been
there. And even now, in your suffering, I am here. I have
not changed.

The Son promised he would not leave you comfortless,
so he sent me to you. Let me be your Comforter. I will not
leave you to walk in the dark. Draw near to me and allow
me to guide you. I will neither hide my face nor will I hide
my Word. Even if everything else in your life changes, you
can trust me to be faithful to you.

Receive my comfort. Just as I sent the prophet Isaiah
with the good news of a Deliverer, so I am sending you to
share this message of my faithfulness with someone else
who feels alone.

**Read
Isaiah 48:12–17.**

*Lord, I am grateful that
you are faithful.*

JANUARY 16

You will receive power when the Holy Spirit comes on you; and you will be my witnesses.

—**Acts 1:8** (NIV)

POWER SUPPLY

They were eleven ordinary men who left everything to follow the Messiah. Before Jesus ascended into heaven, he told them that I would come and give them my power. I did, and the disciples became the most well-known witnesses in history.

I still work this way today. When you ask for my help, I give it. I can strengthen you to be my witness, to reach people near and far for the kingdom.

Do not be discouraged when the world labels you as weak because you trust Jesus. You may feel weak, but I am your source of strength. You may feel inadequate, but I am more than enough for you. Go and be my witness to your world.

Read Acts 1:4–8.

Holy Spirit, I need your power. Help me to be an effective witness.

JANUARY 17

They were all filled with the Holy Spirit and continued to speak the word of God with boldness.

—**Acts 4:31** (ESV)

SPEAK BOLDLY

Child, do you think that I don't hear the threats of those who intimidate you, those who despise me? I allow them to intimidate you as a reminder for you to pray. The Christian community in first-century Jerusalem prayed for courage in the midst of threats from the Jewish council. They did not ask for their burdens to be taken away, for they understood they would endure hardships because they proclaimed the name of Jesus. They asked for boldness to witness and for God to continue doing miracles. With my encouragement, they continued to speak openly and boldly.

In the same way I dwelled in them, I began to dwell in you the moment you gave your life to Jesus. Your prayers were heard then as now. I will continue to be with you always.

Read Acts 4:23–31.

Do not be afraid, and remember I am with you always.

JANUARY 18

*Peter said to them, "Repent, and each of you be baptized in the name of Jesus Christ for the forgiveness of your sins; and you will receive the gift of the Holy Spirit." —*Acts 2:38 (NASB)

NO STRINGS ATTACHED

There once was a chasm between you and the Father. Jesus' sacrifice for your sins bridged that gap, as the apostle Peter told his listeners on the day I arrived on earth. It made my advent into your life possible.

Many are fond of giving gifts with strings attached—hidden costs. The gift of my presence cannot be earned—it is freely and fully offered to you without obligation. Along with my presence, I offer you a full pardon from the penalty of sin, new life, and the strength to live in a way that pleases God. These gifts are yours forever.

Child, I long for you to be free from the sin of this world and filled with grace. Just ask me, and I will renew you. No strings attached.

Read
Acts 2:38–40.

Father, thank you for changing my life. Help me turn from sin to your loving arms.

JANUARY 19

We are witnesses of these things; and so is the Holy Spirit, whom God has given to those who obey Him.

—**Acts 5:32** (NASB)

STANDING TOGETHER

I heard Paul and the apostles teaching people about Jesus' death and resurrection. How he could forgive sins. And then I heard the threats. I saw the high priest's anger. I felt the blows.

When Jesus' followers talk about him today, they are persecuted in more subtle ways. People give them a look, make fun of them, or simply turn away. I see that too.

When people don't believe your testimony, I am with you. When questions assail your assertions of Jesus as Savior, I stand with you. When others doubt the promise and hope of Jesus, I testify with you.

So unslump your shoulders, child. Hold your head high. I know you're trying to obey the Father. Let me be your confidence. No need to be ashamed. What you know is truth. I am a witness to it too. Lock arms with me. We'll keep on the journey and face the opposition together.

**Read
Acts 5:17–42.**

Holy Spirit, please give me courage and stand with me today as I testify of Jesus.

JANUARY 20

Peter told him, "May your silver be destroyed with you, because you thought the gift of God could be obtained with money!"

—**Acts 8:20** (HCSB)

FREELY GIVEN

People say that money makes the world go around. People strive for money as if money can do anything—including buying happiness or a way to be right with God. That was Simon the sorcerer's problem. So impressed was he by my power exhibited through Peter and John that he wanted to buy that power! He wanted to be able to help people receive me, but he did not understand that this ability is not for sale.

I give my gifts when God's people have their hearts right with him. When you receive the gift of Jesus' sacrifice on the cross on your behalf, then I will enter you and bring my gifts for you to share with the world.

No amount of money can buy that.

Read Acts 8:9–24.

Thank you that your gifts are free when my heart is right with you.

JANUARY 21

On the Gentiles also was poured out the gift of the Holy Ghost.

—**Acts 10:45** (KJV)

ALL BELIEVERS ARE WELCOME

When Jesus paved the way of salvation, this precious gift came with the promise of another: the gift of my presence. I am with you, dear child, just as I was with those who listened to the preaching of the apostle Peter.

I am the gift who lets you know beyond any doubt that you are held and hidden within the Father's gentle hands. Through me, God's strength can be yours, my love can burn within you, and you can know with certainty that you are not alone.

Beyond being woven into the mighty plans and purpose of the Almighty, there's another benefit: you are one with every believer around the globe. Every tribe and nation, women and men, young and old—all are part of my family.

Read Acts 10:44–48.

Help me rejoice in the connection of believers. Draw me ever nearer.

Now after he had seen the vision, immediately we sought to go to Macedonia, concluding that the Lord had called us to preach the gospel to them.

—**Acts 16:10** (NKJV)

A THREE-DIMENSIONAL NUDGE

Have you sensed my nudging? I promise it is there in the comfort, discernment, and conviction I help you glean from Scripture. It's in the words of the Savior that I bring to mind just when you need them the most. It's in the ways I direct circumstances and experiences.

Paul felt my nudging on his missionary journeys. One time I used a dream in the middle of the night to give him direction and passion for a preaching trip to Philippi in Macedonia. And when he got there, rejoicing and blessing abounded. People in Philippi believed the message and were saved—all because Paul opened his mind to what I showed him in a vision and then followed my leading.

Are you open to my guidance? It's there, I promise. Look for it today. Look for me today. I'm ready to guide you.

Read Acts 16:6–10.

Help me to be open to your message, Holy Spirit, and not to discount your guidance.

JANUARY 23

*Then the L<small>ORD</small> summoned
me and said, "Look, those
who went north have vented
the anger of my Spirit there
in the land of the north."*
—**Zechariah 6:8** (NLT)

TOUGH LOVE

Beloved, I am the Spirit of truth and comfort. I am
the Spirit of holiness and joy. I am the means by
which those who are weak find strength to face what they
fear most. All the same, I am not a pushover. It is my
nature to stand up for what is right. I am the means by
which people get a fair shake.

When Zechariah had a vision of the four chariots
going to the ends of the earth, he saw me headed with
the black horses in a northerly direction. I couldn't help
myself. The Father's reputation was being soiled and
innocent people were being shamed. My anger could not
be contained. It had to be expressed. You might call it
tough love. Perhaps even costly grace.

It is my desire that your spirit will be grieved by
what grieves me. Righteous indignation is an indicator
that compassion fills your heart.

Read
Zechariah 6:1–8.

*Help me to be angry at the
right time for the right
reasons.*

JANUARY 24

I will place My Spirit within you and cause you to follow My statutes and carefully observe My ordinances.

—**Ezekiel 36:27** (HCSB)

HEART TRANSPLANT

Call me a heart surgeon if you like. That's what I do. I remove hardened, diseased hearts and replace them with ones that are supple and soft. I know how difficult it is for you to function the way you want to when what makes you tick is not working right. You struggle to breathe pure air. Your good intentions tire easily. You stumble on the paths of righteousness. It pains you to admit you aren't the person others think you are.

But, dear one, I love you too much to let you struggle on. The new heart I have for you will allow you to keep pace with God's purposes. This heart will beat in sync with our will. You will have a true desire to please us. Isn't that great news? You will run and not be weary. You will walk and not faint.

Read Ezekiel 36:25–27.

When your desires are the source of my desires, life is worth living.

JANUARY 25

Be wise as serpents and innocent as doves. . . . It is not you who speak, but the Spirit of your Father speaking through you.

—Matthew 10:16, 20 (ESV)

CUNNING

Beloved, I know the thought of being my witness is intimidating to you sometimes. You fear that your tongue will tangle or that you will lack the right words to persuade someone to turn to Jesus. Do you not know that I am the power behind your words?

I can give you the wisdom and the innocence you need to convey my message to a world desperately in need. Just as Jesus sent his disciples, so I send you. But I don't send you alone: I will go with you. Just as I was with those disciples, just as I was with Moses long before them, I will be with you, giving you the right words to use. Just be willing.

Read Matthew 10.

Father, I'm willing to be cunning. Not for my own devices, but for your love and peace.

If you then, being evil, know how to give good gifts to your children, how much more will your heavenly Father give the Holy Spirit to those who ask Him?

—**Luke 11:13** (NASB)

THE GIFT OF THE SPIRIT

We love to give you gifts. The Father, Son, and I take joy in giving you the things that help you, that give you pleasure, and that meet your needs in a way only we can provide. These are the best gifts—the ones you need, want, and cannot possibly get for yourself.

The Son was sent to bridge the gap between you and us; and when his job was done, he sent me to be with you, to help and sustain you through everything else. You do not need to try to make it through life on your own. I am here with you on the earth.

I am the Helper when you need help. I am the Comforter when you want comfort. Nowhere else can you possibly find the assistance that I provide. I love being this gift to you. Pray. When you ask for help, I will provide.

Read
Luke 11:5–13.

Thank you for freely giving me the gift of your Holy Spirit.

*For the one whom God has
sent speaks the words of
God, for God gives the Spirit
without limit.*

—John 3:34 (NIV)

WITHOUT LIMIT

No matter how scary or uncomfortable it may seem to you, do not be afraid when you sense me urging you to take a risk. You are not alone; I am always with you. Although what you're asked to do may appear daunting, I will never give you a task that you cannot accomplish with my help. You will always have my full, limitless attention.

When you feel intimidated or frightened, just lean on me and keep moving forward. Moses felt overwhelmed when he was sent to speak to the pharaoh of Egypt, but the promise of my presence was his. I guided Moses and Aaron in the words they spoke.

When you step out in faith to do my will, I will meet you too, and amaze you with the results. You honor me when you trust me.

Read
John 3:22–36.

*Help me to remember that
your Spirit is always with
me.*

JANUARY 28

There is therefore now no condemnation to those who are in Christ Jesus, who do not walk according to the flesh, but according to the Spirit.

—**Romans 8:1** (NKJV)

NOT GUILTY

Beloved, I have seen many swallow the lie that when you fail, you will always be condemned. They pile up stones of guilt that weigh down their souls.

I have come to relieve you of such burdens. I know you sometimes give in to temptation, child. My mission is not to nail you to the cross that took Jesus' life. His was a once-for-all-time gift of such enormity that even today women and men struggle to comprehend its reach and gravity. They choose to cling to guilt rather than to God.

I bring life to you through your faith in Jesus. Laws exist to force people toward righteousness. Know me, and understand that Jesus' beautiful sacrifice brings you life—not condemnation. Rejoice!

Read Romans 8:1–4.

Help me to hear the Holy Spirit's voice and guide me in paths of righteousness.

JANUARY 29

*These things we also speak,
not in words which man's
wisdom teaches but which the
Holy Spirit teaches, comparing
spiritual things with spiritual.*

—1 Corinthians 2:13 (NKJV)

BRINGING UNDERSTANDING

When children are young and have no understanding of language, their parents communicate with them in ways that transcend words. A smile, a hug, a kiss, rocking in a chair, moments of cuddling, and times of feeding or humming lullabies send messages to an infant that he is safe, loved, and protected.

So I too, without words, speak of the majesty of God. By presenting myriad stars, roaring oceans, and towering redwoods, I reveal the creative divinity of the Almighty. By calming the heart during times of anxiety, I speak of peace from the Master. By opening the mind to a deeper understanding of the Scriptures, I speak of the wisdom of the immortal. My messages are given with spiritual language, understood instinctively by those who are akin to my nature.

Read
1 Corinthians
2:10–16.

*Holy Spirit, let me attune
my ear to your righteous
message.*

JANUARY 30

God chose you as the firstfruits to be saved, through sanctification by the Spirit and belief in the truth.

—2 Thessalonians 2:13 (ESV)

THE SPIRIT SANCTIFIES

In earthly realms, when the first son of a king is born, it is announced on the day of his birth that he is destined to be the future king—to one day have a crown placed on his head, a scepter put in his hand, and a royal robe draped over his shoulders. It is predestined that one day he will rule a vast kingdom and that all the people therein will be subject to his will and commands.

So it is that I, from the beginning, have preordained that those who love and serve God shall be adorned with a crown of salvation and shall be robed eternally with truth, understanding, and wisdom in all things righteous and spiritual. Because I, the Spirit, have adorned the redeemed with a soul that is ever increasing in holiness, it is proper that God be praised for his mercy and divine blessings on all who are submissive to his will and commands.

You have been chosen to receive sanctification—to grow in holiness, to become more like the Savior. You are chosen and destined! Live like it!

Read
2 Thessalonians
2:6–17.

I praise the Almighty for providing salvation and drawing me ever closer to him.

The Spirit and the bride say, "Come." And let the one who hears say, "Come." And let the one who is thirsty come; let the one who wishes take the water of life without cost.

—**Revelation 22:17** (NASB)

WELCOMING BELIEVERS TO HEAVEN

On earth, travelers who venture over a vast desert quickly discover the misery of unrelenting heat, stinging sand, and desolate landscape. All too soon they have a desperate craving for protective shade and cool water, but all they encounter are dunes, dry winds, and a barren horizon. If by a miracle they see an oasis in the distance and hear welcome calls from other pilgrims, encouraging them to join them in wells of refreshment, they stumble forward, seeking the renewing waters.

In like manner, I, the Holy One who offers spiritual nourishment in abundance, call the welcoming word, "Come!" I have gushing streams, tumbling waterfalls, and overflowing wells of living water. When you are thirsty, I implore you to drink freely, immersing yourselves in the eternal fountain of God's grace, love, and care.

Read Revelation 22:12–21.

Holy Spirit, fill my cup this day with living water.

FEBRUARY

The Character of the Spirit

FEBRUARY 1

*If you respond to my warning,
then I will pour out my spirit
on you and teach you my
words.*

—**Proverbs 1:23** (HCSB)

AN OUTPOURING OF THE SPIRIT

Child, the time you spend learning from me is very precious. Sometimes, when you are in a hurry, you only have a few minutes to read some Scripture and pray. Other days, you read leisurely, take notes, have a second cup of coffee, and pray for everyone you know.

I am glad that you make the effort. Don't let our times together become just another obligation to fulfill. As you grow in your faith, you will know my leading. When you humbly respond to my reproof, I am able to pour myself into you and fill the empty spaces. Your understanding of my will increases, bringing deeper love and awe of your Creator.

Cherish these times spent alone with me. Heaven rejoices every time you do.

**Read
Proverbs 1:20–23.**

*Help me not to neglect
my daily time with you!
Thank you for all you
provide through my
devotional times.*

FEBRUARY 2

He will baptize you with the
Holy Spirit and with fire.

—**Matthew 3:11** (NLT)

BAPTISM BY FIRE

The term *baptism by fire* has come to mean putting oneself into a difficult situation and hoping for the best. Yet when John the Baptist talked about baptism by fire, he had a very different definition in mind.

John was our servant, who I filled while he was still in his mother's womb. When he baptized people, he did so with water, a symbol of washing away past sins. When Jesus stood before John, waiting for baptism, John was befuddled. Jesus was sinless! Yet he chose to be baptized as an example for all sinful people.

John recognized he had no power to forgive sins— water baptism only symbolizes one's repentance. When Jesus baptizes with fire, his power of forgiveness burns away the sins of the past; the repentant one then receives my filling. A true baptism of the Holy Spirit and fire!

Read
Matthew 3:1–11.

I repent of my sins!
Please burn them up and
baptize me with the Holy
Spirit.

He who believes in Me, as the Scripture said, "From his innermost being will flow rivers of living water." But this He spoke of the Spirit.

—John 7:38–39 (NASB)

LIVING WATER

Child, do you thirst for righteousness and long to be filled? Are you a desert wishing for streams of living water?

If you truly believe in Jesus—not just as head knowledge, but with your whole heart, believing he is your Savior—then out of your heart will flow living water. I have filled you to overflowing! As I bubble over into every facet of your life, you cannot help but share what God has done to you, for you, and through you.

Draw your friends near to me by allowing them to see the rivers of living water that I have brought to you. Watch as their lives are transformed. Marvel at the power of my waters flowing through the humble vessel of your transformed heart.

Read John 7:37–39.

Help me share with others the powerful living water of your Spirit within my heart.

FEBRUARY 4

I will pray the Father, and he
shall give you another Comforter
. . . even the Spirit of truth.

—John 14:16–17 (KJV)

SPIRIT OF TRUTH

The truth is important, isn't it? You want to know the truth. When someone speaks to you, you hope that you can count on what he or she is saying to be true. In fact, you generally assume it unless you begin to discover the person to be untruthful.

Beloved one, I *am* the Spirit of truth. I am in your life to reveal the truth and expose lies, deceit, confusion, and false teachings. I want you to know what is true, to know what to trust, to know that you can count on me to provide direction to righteousness, benevolence, and oneness with God.

Christ has promised my presence to all who trust in his words, and so I come now, the Spirit of truth, giving you wisdom that only the One known as "the way" and "the truth" can bestow.

Read
John 14:11–20.

Allow me now, divine
Spirit, to accept the full
measure of truth you
offer me.

FEBRUARY 5

The Helper, the Holy Spirit, whom the Father will send in My name, He will teach you all things, and bring to your remembrance all that I said to you. —**John 14:26** (NASB)

OUR SPIRITUAL TEACHER

Jesus, most appropriately, was called Teacher, Lord, Master, and Prophet. His sermons and lessons and stories opened the eyes of seekers. In simple yet profound ways, he explained our will to all who approached him— shepherds, carpenters, tax collectors, fishermen, lawyers, scribes, priests, soldiers, politicians, businessmen. As a youth, he sat among the temple rabbis and explained the Scriptures. In the wilderness he thwarted Satan by quoting the holy writ aloud. On the mount he shared new commandments with the multitudes gathered there.

Now, I am sent to burn his words on your memory. I am called to show the application of his teachings to life's daily challenges. I am the Spirit who makes obvious the practicality of the Master's lessons. I am here for you, to teach you righteous living and holy teachings.

Read
John 14:20–31.

Holy One, as I read the Scriptures, instill your wisdom and discernment in me.

FEBRUARY 6

All of Mount Sinai was covered with smoke because the LORD had descended on it in the form of fire.

—**Exodus 19:18** (NLT)

A HUMBLING REMINDER

Just two months after Moses led the Israelites out of Egypt, they paused at the base of Mount Sinai. Moses called the people to prepare for a dramatic, divine encounter. They needed to be reminded to whom they belonged. They had not freed themselves; they could not care for themselves en route to the land promised them. They were chosen people, with a holy, untouchable God.

I appeared as fire on the mountain. It was my way of getting the people's attention. My flames warned Israel not to come too close. But my flames also reminded them in no uncertain terms that I was with them and that I would care for them.

I have chosen you as well. You are special to me. But do not think of me as your equal. I am the holy God who demands honor and worship.

Read
Exodus 19:16–20.

I approach you gratefully and humbly, for you are the Mighty One.

FEBRUARY 7

The Spirit of God has made me, and the breath of the Almighty gives me life.

—Job 33:4 (NKJV)

THE LIFE GIVER

Breathe in deeply. Smell the freshness of the air after a rain. Feel the kiss of the sun on your face after a long winter. Listen to the symphony of birds as they herald the breaking of a new day. Look around you. All living things, from the tiniest insects to the most magnificent of my creatures, are instilled with my life-giving breath. Behold the wonders and beauty of life itself!

You too, child, are an expression of this very same life source—unique and wonderfully made, precious to me. I have given you not only life and breath but also the ability to enjoy and to care for my creation.

This very day is my gift to you. How will you use today? What will you do to reflect your Creator to those around you?

Read
Job 33:4.

Thank you, Holy Spirit, for the gift of life this day. Help me to honor you in how I live today.

FEBRUARY 8

When you send your Spirit, they are created, and you renew the face of the ground.

—**Psalm 104:30** (NIV)

RENEWAL

Each spring, from the dead of winter, life rises anew. Each sprout, every bud, every emerging stalk is the promise of renewal. It is my greatest joy to see life revived and restored. Just as the nation of Israel was restored from exile back to their homeland, as Jonah was offered a fresh start after running away, as Ezekiel prophesied in his vision seeing dead bones come back to life, I offer renewal to all who turn to me. It is the very message of the gospel—new life offered through the blood and sacrifice of God the Son.

Where do you need revitalization today? Is it due to following a wrong path? An estrangement with a loved one? A spiritual life that has gone dry? I am there, waiting to breathe new life into every situation you experience today.

Read Psalm 104.

Holy Spirit, renew me today. Refresh my spirit and restore me to a right relationship with God.

FEBRUARY 9

After Jesus was baptized, He went up immediately from the water. The heavens suddenly opened for Him, and He saw the Spirit of God descending like a dove and coming down on Him.
—**Matthew 3:16** (HCSB)

THREE IN ONE

The time had come. The Son had been tried and tested; his path was laid out before him. Only one course of action remained: baptism. So he went from Galilee to the Jordan River where his cousin John was baptizing repentant sinners, preparing the way for the Messiah. At first John demurred, but Jesus gently insisted, "Allow it for now, because this is the way for us to fulfill all righteousness" (Matthew 3:15 HCSB). And so it was.

At that very moment when Jesus came up from the water, I descended upon him like a dove, confirming that he, indeed, was the Messiah. Like a proud parent, the Father affirmed, "This is My beloved Son. I take delight in Him!" (Matthew 3:17 HCSB).

Dear one, know that wherever the Father and Son are at work, so am I. And whoever the Father has called and given to the Son, I am there also. Three working as one.

Read
Matthew 3:16–17.

I don't fully understand the Trinity. But I accept that you are with me—three acting as one.

FEBRUARY 10

*But I tell you the truth, it is to
your advantage that I go away;
for if I do not go away, the
Helper will not come to you; but
if I go, I will send Him to you.*

—**John 16:7** (NASB)

THE COMFORTER

It was difficult for the disciples. They couldn't
understand why Jesus had to die, why he had to leave
them. Their hearts were filled with sorrow. But the truth
is that if Jesus remained, I would not be able to come.
Jesus' presence on earth was limited to time and space.
His leaving meant that the entire world could receive him
through me.

I enter into the hearts and lives of every person who
calls upon the name of the Lord. I am with you as your
Helper. Are you confused about which path to take? I am
there; listen for my voice. Do you need strength to get
through a difficult situation? I will never leave your side.
Is your soul weighed down and weary with grief? I will
comfort you.

Even though he had to leave the disciples behind,
they would never be alone. Neither will you, dear child. I
am here—your Helper, Comforter, and Advocate.

**Read
John 16:7.**

*Spirit, Helper,
Comforter, Friend,
make your presence
known to me today
where I most need it.*

FEBRUARY 11

In the same way, the Spirit helps us in our weakness. We do not know what we ought to pray for, but the Spirit himself intercedes for us through wordless groans.

—**Romans 8:26** (NIV)

HE INTERCEDES

Child, I not only help you pray, but I pray *for* you. On the days when you're racked with pain or feel lost and confused and can only groan, I interpret the very groans you utter. I help you turn your eyes to the Father, even when you're too weak to pray.

As our servant Paul wrote, sometimes you don't know what to pray. You might ask for what you think is best, little knowing that what you believe is best is actually the worst thing for you. I have an intimate connection with every feeling you've ever felt.

I know what you need; rely on me today to plead on your behalf. I always have your best interests at heart.

Read
Romans 8:22–27.

Holy Spirit, please be the words I am searching to find in prayer.

FEBRUARY 12

You are not in the flesh but in the Spirit, if indeed the Spirit of God dwells in you. Now if anyone does not have the Spirit of Christ, he is not His.

—**Romans 8:9** (NKJV)

REBUILDING YOU

When I entered your life, you were like a decaying house—in need of repair. You needed me, but you didn't know how much. Yet your realization of your sin and brokenness, your love and need for the Savior, put me into action.

Because you belong to Jesus, I went straight to work, rooting out attitudes and behaviors that are harmful to you and to others. I have a plan, child—a plan to make you fit for heaven. Knowing how beautiful you will become as you rely on me for the renovations of your soul brings me joy.

I know this work isn't comfortable and makes you angry with me sometimes. On this side of heaven, you won't understand how much I love you. But I love you too much to stop the work of rebuilding you.

Read Romans 8:5–11.

Spirit, I welcome your new life into my creaky soul.

FEBRUARY 13

Take the helmet of salvation,
and the sword of the Spirit,
which is the word of God.

—**Ephesians 6:17** (KJV)

UNSHEATHE ME

When thick, murky fog obstructs your vision, I can pierce it. When you are lost in a jungle of trials, I can chop through it. In the midst of your situation today, you are not powerless. I am here. I've been in your life since the day you believed in Jesus.

Child of God, unsheath my sword—your defense and offense. The hilt has been perfectly crafted to complement the shape of your hand, the curve of your fingers, and the weight of your arm. Wield my Word against the trials, pain, and sorrow. When weariness comes and your mind tells you that lifting an arm is impossible, just call to me. I will fit the sword of the Word to you so it is exactly what you need today.

Read
Ephesians 6:10–18.

Thank you for giving me your sword—the Word of God—to use in life's battles.

Worship God! For it is the Spirit of prophecy who bears testimony to Jesus.

—**Revelation 19:10** (NIV)

READY TO SHARE

I gave our servant John amazing visions of the end times, and the angels gave him instructions. So overwhelmed was John that he fell down in worship of the angel, but the angel promptly refused worship, directing John to exalt God alone. The angel was a servant, just like those other believers in John's vision—and just like you.

As our servant, you also are "prophesying," for you are bearing testimony to Jesus and what he has done in your life. Prophecy is not just telling the future (although it can mean that); it is giving a clear witness about Jesus. Because of his death on the cross, I can be in your life, helping you share that testimony.

Let me show you who needs to hear your story, and then let me help you tell it.

Read Revelation 19:1–10.

Help me to share my story with those who are ready to hear about Jesus.

FEBRUARY 15

The Spirit of the LORD will rest on Him—a Spirit of wisdom and understanding, a Spirit of counsel and strength, a Spirit of knowledge and of the fear of the LORD.

—Isaiah 11:2 (HCSB)

RESOURCED

Eight hundred years before Jesus was born, a prophet named Isaiah described the qualities that would mark God's Messiah. To the human eye he would look just like any ordinary first-century Jew. But appearances are deceiving. Jesus was hardly an ordinary man. He was truly unique. It was I who fully inhabited him. Even as human blood flowed through his veins, I animated the life of his soul.

I filled Jesus with heavenly wisdom. I opened his ears and his heart so he could understand those he observed. It was I who infused his mind with the ability to respond to what he understood. I gave him the ability to fully obey his Father. And, child, that is what I desire to do for you. In the frantic pace of your day, won't you quiet yourself now and allow me to rest on you?

Read
Isaiah 11:1–9.

If Jesus needed to be fully inhabited by you, I need you all the more to equip me for today.

FEBRUARY 16

He gave me the priestly duty of proclaiming the gospel of God, so that the Gentiles might become an offering acceptable to God, sanctified by the Holy Spirit.

—**Romans 15:16** (NIV)

YOU ARE ACCEPTABLE

Child, I've changed you on the inside. I dwell in you to bring you hope. I know you're on a journey that sometimes gets tough. Like a baseball player sliding into home plate just under the catcher's mitt, you can get covered in dust. And no matter what the umpire's call, a coach or parent on the sidelines is bound to disagree with it. But the umpire has the final say. I'm that umpire. Ignore those around you who are just trying to pick a fight. Focus on me, and be encouraged.

Remember what I've done for you. Remember who I am. And remember who you are—saved through Christ, acceptable and made holy by me.

Read
Romans 15:13–16.

O God, help me to believe your call to holiness and acceptance.

FEBRUARY 17

At that moment the Spirit of the LORD came powerfully upon him, and he ripped the lion's jaws apart with his bare hands.

—**Judges 14:6** (NLT)

STRENGTH AS NEEDED

I was there when Samson was traveling with his parents to introduce them to a woman who caught his fancy. I knew that he was caught off guard when a lion leaped from the grape vineyards and tried to devour him. It was I who filled Samson with the strength to wrestle the beast to the ground and break his neck. Though some might think his strength was in his uncut hair, I was Samson's source of empowerment.

Samson had been dedicated to a holy cause. As Scripture reveals, he didn't always live in a holy manner, but he had access to my power. That's great news, isn't it? Your need of my help is not dependent on your perfection.

I am here to empower you for the "wild beasts" that threaten you. They may not be literal lions, but they are just as frightening. Whenever you need help, just call on me for strength.

Read Judges 14:6, 19; 15:14.

Help me to call on you for strength when I feel weak.

FEBRUARY 18

The Holy Spirit said, "Set apart for Me Barnabas and Saul for the work to which I have called them."

—Acts 13:2 (NASB)

BETTER THAN CONFETTI!

It was a send-off even better than the confetti, blowers, and whistles when a ship leaves port for its maiden voyage. Even better than the hugs, nail biting, and waves of your family when you back out of the driveway for the first time with your new driver's license. Even better than throwing rice at the bride and groom leaving on their honeymoon.

It was a prayer, a blessing, a commendation. That's what I did for Barnabas and Saul before they went to Cyprus to preach the gospel. I whispered that the time had come. Barnabas and Saul were ready. The work was ready. The church was ready. I commissioned the journey.

Draw close. Lean on me. I'm still a "commissioner." Keep focusing on the tasks I have already planned for you today, even as you wait, like Barnabas and Saul, for what I have for you tomorrow. And if a time comes for a longer journey, you can count on me to give you the perfect send-off.

Read
Acts 13:2–4.

Lord, grant me the desire to trust you for each day's mission.

FEBRUARY 19

Living in the fear of the Lord and encouraged by the Holy Spirit, [the church] increased in numbers.

—**Acts 9:31** (NIV)

THE SPIRIT OF ENCOURAGEMENT

Saul of Tarsus was a great sinner, a persecutor of God's children. Many were skeptical when they heard the news of his conversion. Many were terrified when he came into Jerusalem. But I used his salvation to encourage the church. The believers' stamina increased as they realized there was nothing more to fear from Saul. When they saw that even such a man as he could be changed, I inspired them to reach out to others. Many more believed. The church grew stronger and larger through my encouragement, and I was most pleased to see believers' faith grow also.

My work as an encourager is far from over. My desire is to increase the faith of every child of God. I am here for you every day, loved one, to calm your fears and to give you strength to endure times of hardship and temptation. Let me be your peace today.

Read Acts 9:20–31.

Spirit, let me look to you for encouragement each day. Amen.

FEBRUARY 20

A spiritual gift is given to each of us so we can help each other.

—**1 Corinthians 12:7** (NLT)

NO ASSEMBLY REQUIRED

My hands are outstretched to you today, filled with a gift I chose just for you. Go ahead, take this gift. I want you to have it. It doesn't need batteries; it doesn't need to be assembled. It's complete, ready to use just as it is.

Beloved, giving gifts is a joy for me. Wisdom, knowledge, discernment—I delight to give these gifts that are so much a part of who I am. I love seeing the fuller worship that comes as a result of each child using his or her gifts to benefit others.

I picked your spiritual gift especially for you to use for the common good. Bless your brothers and sisters in Christ with your gift. Ask me how. I can help you.

Read
1 Corinthians 12:4–11.

Thank you, heavenly Father, for my spiritual gift. Help me use it wisely to benefit other believers.

FEBRUARY 21

Those who are led by the Spirit of God are the children of God.

—**Romans 8:14** (NIV)

LOVING LEADERSHIP

Beloved, I can help you make prudent decisions each day about who you will follow. I have seen many people scurry after those in the spotlight. Others follow their own selfish desires. But many have chosen to take on the burden of the cross and pursue Jesus.

I know these faithful believers by name and gladly lead those who call God their Father. Take my hand, child, and I will show you righteous paths and guide you through darkness. For I am the Spirit of God. I am here because I was sent to give you strength and comfort.

I can lift your heart from the grip of fear. With my touch, my leading, you will remember to whom you belong. Take heed, precious child. I lead you because you are loved.

**Read
Romans 8:12–17.**

Let the light of the Holy Spirit lead me to the grace of the Savior.

Anyone with ears to hear must listen to the Spirit and understand what he is saying to the churches.

—**Revelation 2:7** (NLT)

USE YOUR EARS TO LISTEN

Glorious news! Can you hear the trumpets? I come to those of you who hunger, who never feel full. I have seen your patience in the face of painful struggle. I know you have endured, turned from evil, and worked hard. But the journey is not over.

I am bursting to tell you what will happen at the finish line. You will enjoy the smell, scent, and taste of the fruit from the tree of life—the source of eternal life. Just imagine. You will nibble on nectar-filled bites from the bounteous tree that once towered in Adam and Eve's perfect garden. Picture its leaves unfurled, shiny and strong, its limbs bowed with luscious fruit for you to sample.

Life eternal will be your victory, faithful one. I, the Spirit, say once more, listen to the promise of what God has prepared for you: a fruitful feast forever!

Read Revelation 2:1–7.

Keep my ears open that I may always listen to your Spirit.

FEBRUARY 23

We impart this in words not taught by human wisdom but taught by the Spirit, interpreting spiritual truths to those who are spiritual.

—**1 Corinthians 2:13** (ESV)

TEACHER

Christians in this world aren't alone. I am the guide God has given to help you discern between the wisdom of this age and that which is greater.

Since you are saved, you and your brothers and sisters in Christ are different. You've been called to do different things. You've been called to have different values. You've also been called to have different knowledge: the knowledge I've given you.

Our ways are above man's ways. But because of me, you get to know things others can't possibly imagine. This knowledge is different from the knowledge men prize. Our ways are infinitely more wonderful.

I am with you for a purpose. I want you to "understand the things freely given . . . by God" (1 Corinthians 2:12 ESV). This includes spiritual knowledge much richer than anything this world can offer.

Let me teach you.

Read
1 Corinthians
2:6–16.

Dear Father, help me trust you to teach me spiritual things.

*I will send you the Advocate—
the Spirit of truth. He will come
to you from the Father and will
testify all about me.*

—**John 15:26** (NLT)

SPIRIT OF TRUTH

Jesus told his followers that he would send me, calling me an advocate (or other Bible versions use the term *counselor* or *helper*). And that is what I am: your Advocate, your Helper, your Counselor who is there to encourage and strengthen you. When Jesus returned to heaven, he sent me to be there for you, *in* you, so you would never be alone.

You never have to doubt the truth of all Jesus says because I am also the Spirit of truth. I teach, illuminate, and remind you of what you learn in reading God's Word, of what you've been taught, of what I've taught you through your past experiences.

I am here as the Spirit of truth so you can be assured that all I remind you about the Father and the Son is true—forever.

Read John 15. *Spirit of truth, guide me into your truth.*

FEBRUARY 25

And shall put my spirit in you, and ye shall live, and I shall place you in your own land: then shall ye know that I the LORD have spoken it, and performed it, saith the LORD.

—Ezekiel 37:14 (KJV)

THE BREATH OF GOD

Beloved, after his creation, man became a living soul through the breath I provided. From the very start, Adam was a spiritual being. Just as you require oxygen to live, so you cannot live life to the fullest without the breath of life I provide.

I know that hard times have a way of deflating you, child. But I can restore you. The prophet Ezekiel recorded the promise of my presence in the restoration of Israel after the ordeal of exile. Just as God's people would once again return to their land, restored through my power, so I can restore you after any devastating circumstance. What a wonderful thought!

No matter your circumstance right now, I am as near to you as your next breath.

Read
Ezekiel 37:9–14.

You are the air I breathe. As I inhale and exhale I will remind myself that you are with me.

*When he, the Spirit of truth,
comes, he will guide you into
all the truth.*

—**John 16:13** (NIV)

TRUTH WILL GUIDE YOU

The Son of God promised his disciples and all who
follow him that I, the Spirit of truth, would be with
them. I am with you not only to show the truth but also to
"guide you into all the truth." Yet the truth I speak to you
is not from me. It is from the Father. All truth comes from
the Father.

It is through me that you receive the truth of the
Father. It is through me that the Father crafts you into an
excellent witness for the Son. When you are guided into
all truth, you can know for certain that everything written
in God's Word can be counted on. You need never wonder
about the future, about your pathway in life, about the joys
and suffering you face—for you have the truth.

And that, dear child, is all you need.

Read
John 16:12–15.

*Help me to cling to
and learn the Father's
truth that the Spirit
teaches me.*

FEBRUARY 27

[The Spirit] will bring me glory by telling you whatever he receives from me.

—John 16:14 (NLT)

I WILL TEACH YOU

Jesus talked a lot about me as the time drew closer to his crucifixion, preparing his followers for what at the time surely seemed impossible to them—his continued presence after he was gone. This would happen through my presence in the life of every individual believer.

You see, when I am in your life, I bring you the truth of the Father and the Son. I teach you all that they want you to know. I help you understand the teachings of Scripture and, because I am intimately involved in your life, I show you how to apply those teachings to your specific situation.

Beloved, I know what you're going through today. I am here to help.

Read John 16:5–15.

As I read your Word today, teach me what I need to know and show me how to apply it.

FEBRUARY 28

*The Lord—who is the Spirit—
makes us more and more like
him as we are changed into his
glorious image.*

—**2 Corinthians 3:18** (NLT)

MYSTERIOUS TRINITY

The Trinity is a cosmic mystery. The Father, Son,
and I are all one, yet distinct. Your human mind
cannot comprehend this, but that should actually make
you glad. If you could figure it all out, then it would cease
to be a mystery. And you need that mystery. You need
to know that we are greater than your mind can begin to
understand. You need a God beyond and outside you.

If God were small enough to be understood, he
wouldn't be big enough to be God.

Here's an even greater mystery: as you draw close
to us, you become more and more like us. We help you to
become more like us in our glory. And one day, when you
see us face to face, you will be complete, perfect.

Read
2 Corinthians 3:7–18.

*I may not understand
everything about the
Trinity, but I trust in
your promises.*

MARCH

THE WORK OF THE SPIRIT

The earth was without form, and void; and darkness was on the face of the deep. And the Spirit of God was hovering over the face of the waters.

—**Genesis 1:2** (NKJV)

IN THE BEGINNING . . .

In the beginning, we three were there: Father, Son, and Holy Spirit. Three in one person, one in purpose.

Before the earth was created, I hovered over the waters that were dark, still, and empty. Creation began, not with a purposeless collision of atoms but with a word. With such magnificent power, words that were simply spoken became tangible elements of life.

For five days, only words were used to create. On the sixth day, I took the dust and lovingly crafted the prototype of all humanity, breathing into man and bringing immediate consciousness and life.

Yes, we three were there. And since the dawn of creation until now, we have been involved in every intricate part of the creation. I once hovered over nothingness; now I fill the souls of all who call Jesus their Lord.

And I will fill you.

Read Genesis 1.

Thank you for creating the first humans, for creating me, and for filling me with your Spirit.

MARCH 2

I will take some of the Spirit that is on you and put it on them, and they shall bear the burden of the people with you, so that you may not bear it yourself alone.

—**Numbers 11:17** (ESV)

MY STRENGTH IN YOUR WEAKNESS

I empowered Moses with wisdom to rule over many. Still, he was only one man limited to twenty-four hours in a day. With so many people complaining to him, he recognized his human limitations and asked God for help. My power was provided to seventy men. When I came upon them, they began to prophesy. With my help, they judged wisely and kept the peace among those in the wilderness.

Dear child, whether you have charge of seventy or seven hundred, or whether you have charge only over yourself, you can count on me for guidance and wisdom. Don't forget to look daily into the Word of God and pray without ceasing to the One who saved you.

When you recognize your limitations and allow me to work through you, you will make wise decisions and accomplish great things.

Read
Numbers 11:1–25.

God, grant me the wisdom and power of the Holy Spirit in my daily decisions.

MARCH 3

You sent Your good Spirit to instruct them. You did not withhold Your manna from their mouths, and You gave them water for their thirst.

—**Nehemiah 9:20** (HCSB)

CLASS IS IN SESSION

Remember when you were very young, learning new things in school? You looked forward to each class, eagerly absorbing each drop of knowledge.

I was a teacher to those who wandered in the wilderness for forty years. I taught many lessons, each tailored to the need of the individual wanderer. My lessons in love, joy, peace, kindness, goodness, faithfulness, gentleness, and especially patience and self-control, are what brought the children of Israel into the Promised Land.

Dear one, do you recognize my teaching each day? Your growth depends upon learning the lessons and applying them to your life. When you look forward to each lesson and eagerly spend time with your Teacher, your heart will become wise.

Read
Nehemiah 9:19–21.

Holy Spirit, I look forward to what you will teach me today.

I have filled [Bezalel] with the Spirit of God, with ability and intelligence, with knowledge and all craftsmanship.

—Exodus 31:3 (ESV)

HEAVENLY ARCHITECT

I am calling you, dear one, to be my hands and feet, to work the works that I have planned.

I gave to Bezalel the talent and skill to do all that would be required of him. I purposefully called him by name. Through me, a sinful man crafted the very dwelling place of God.

Who shaped you in your mother's womb? Who bestowed every ability upon you? Be bold, for I will not abandon you. In the greatest of trials and challenges, I will strengthen and comfort you.

I commissioned Bezalel for the beautiful craftsmanship of the tabernacle, knowing my people would later reject me. Yet I called him so that through the work of his hands, they might know God. And I am calling you to bear my reputation before the world! Allow me to indwell your life so that the nations may see you and worship the Lord.

**Read
Exodus 31:1–11.**

God, please use and shape my abilities to better serve your kingdom.

MARCH 5

Bezalel, Oholiab, and all the skilled people are to work based on everything the LORD has commanded. The LORD has given them wisdom and understanding to know how to do all the work of constructing the sanctuary.

—**Exodus 36:1** (HCSB)

MORE THAN ADEQUATE FOR THE TASK

Beloved of God, I have given you every talent needed to serve me. When Moses brought Bezalel before the people of Israel, I had already filled him with the abilities he needed, and more. I will not embarrass those who bear my name. I am calling you to build my kingdom, and every resource you need will be provided. So do not hesitate, and do not listen to the lies of the enemy. The accusations and whispers of inadequacy are blasphemies against the living God.

I held fast to the men who served me in building the tabernacle. Through the work of their hands, I spoke to my people. What reason do you have to fear, now that the victory over death has been achieved through the Son? My strength upholds you; the enemy lies vanquished at your feet. Come, use your gifts for the glory of God.

Read
Exodus 35:30–36:7.

God, make me one of your skilled workers, building up and instructing others in your ways.

MARCH 6

*The Lord replied to Moses,
"Take Joshua son of Nun, a
man who has the Spirit in
him, and lay your hands on
him."*

—**Numbers 27:18** (HCSB)

ANOINTED TO LEAD

It has long been man's tradition to have an elder put
his hand upon a younger man, anointing him in the
presence of witnesses to signify the transfer of spiritual
power and authority. This was done for Joshua.

I, the conveyor of righteous approval, do more than
lay a hand of symbolic praise on our servants. I enter and
reside within the entire person, imbuing the recipient with
might, purpose, focus, energy, and confidence. It is I who
gives courage to a young boy so that he may slay a giant.
It is I who gives a message to a desert wanderer that he
may proclaim with boldness the coming of the Messiah. It
is I who gives a vision of end times to an exiled disciple
so that he may reveal Jesus as the Alpha and Omega. I
am the abiding Spirit, and I will anoint you for the plans I
have for you.

**Read
Numbers 27:12–23.**

*As a servant of God, I
welcome you within me,
Holy Spirit.*

MARCH 7

*Joshua the son of Nun was full
of the spirit of wisdom, for Moses
had laid his hands on him.*

—**Deuteronomy 34:9** (ESV)

THE SPIRIT OF WISDOM

I make myself ever available to provide wisdom to those
who humbly call upon me. If a person will confess
weakness, I will provide strength. If he will admit limitations, I will expand capabilities. I gave Joshua wisdom as
he took Moses' place as Israel's leader.

The truly wise person recognizes that his power and
insight and discernment are gifts from God and are meant
to be returned to the Almighty through acts of obedience
and service. Other people will observe and then recognize
my blessing upon a person who is wiser than his or her
years. When you are filled with me, others will readily
heed your words and direction, for when the Father, Son,
and I call a servant, we also provide a leader's wisdom.

**Read
Deuteronomy 34:5–12.**

*Lord, I need the wisdom
that you provide. Fill me
today.*

MARCH 8

The Spirit of the LORD came on him, so that he became Israel's judge and went to war.

—**Judges 3:10** (NIV)

YOU ARE A LEADER!

Beloved child, you are a leader. Though the thought may intimidate you, this is the role you were born to fill.

I chose Othniel, the younger brother of Caleb, to become the leader of a disobedient Israel. I led him into battle against overwhelming odds and made him victorious over the enemies who threatened. I can do the same for you.

I know how tempted you are sometimes to minimize your influence in the lives of others due to doubt, fear, or feelings of inadequacy. Take heart, beloved. I will be with you just as I was with Othniel. I will help you manage your time and choose your words. I empower you to lead. Now that should bring a smile to your face.

Read
Judges 3:7–11.

Help me to be empowered by your Spirit to lead in a way that pleases you.

*And Balaam raised his eyes,
and saw Israel encamped
according to their tribes; and the
Spirit of God came upon him.*

—**Numbers 24:2** (NKJV)

LOOK TO ME

I know how easily overwhelmed you feel when you have more tasks than you have hours in the day. When you open your eyes to the demands before you, don't fixate on what you have to do. Instead, look to me. I will fill you with all the fuel you need to do what is most important today.

It is my joy to help you see new ways of doing things. I provide power and steer you in a good direction. But I don't wish to drag you into a new point of view the way a mule is dragged. As with Balaam, don't be limited by what seemed to work previously. Trust me for a better way.

There will be those in your life who will try to get you to settle for less than what's best. Don't buy that lie. Raise your eyes above what is staring you in the face and cast your glance in my direction. Don't curse today. I have blessings to give you.

**Read
Numbers 24:1–9.**

*Lord, instead of fixating
on my to-do list today, I
choose to focus on you, the
Source of my blessings.*

MARCH 10

The Spirit of the LORD will control you, you will prophesy with them, and you will be transformed into a different person.

—1 Samuel 10:6 (HCSB)

NEW OPPORTUNITIES

Dear one, today is another chance to trust me as you face new opportunities and challenges. Remember that I am at work in your life and I have my own timetable. You are a person in process. Sometimes you are tempted to get impatient with your progress. But don't despair. Transformation is my concern. It's what I do best.

When Samuel anointed Saul to be king, I was there to pave the way for a new dimension in his life. He had never prophesied before. But I put thoughts in his head that flowed from his lips. He fit right in with those with whom he worshiped. He didn't have to worry about doing something new. And neither do you, beloved.

As you face things today that cause you to fret, allow me to do what I do best. Don't waste time worrying. I live within you, and I go before you.

Read
1 Samuel 10:6–10.

I am excited to know you will give me the words to say when I'm unsure.

MARCH 11

So Samuel took the horn of oil and anointed him in the presence of his brothers, and from that day on the Spirit of the LORD came powerfully upon David.

—**1 Samuel 16:13** (NIV)

EMPOWERED

Samuel examined all of David's older brothers before considering him. I wouldn't let the prophet rest until he anointed the right choice. Even then, David knew he wasn't qualified to lead Israel; he was the son of a sheep farmer. But I refused to let him question his call. As Samuel emptied the flask of olive oil on David's head, I filled the shepherd's heart with the ability to lead his people.

Though you won't wear the crown of royalty on earth, you are royalty. You are a child of the King of heaven. And there is something meaningful for you to do. When the Father chooses individuals to carry out specific assignments, he doesn't expect them to rely on their own experience or strength any more than he expected David to rely on his.

When you feel weak, trust my strength. I will give you the power you need for today.

Read 1 Samuel 16:6–13.

Lord, help me realize that I have all I need to accomplish the challenges today will bring.

Restore to me the joy of Your
salvation, and uphold me by
Your generous Spirit.

—**Psalm 51:12** (NKJV)

RESTORE MY JOY

David's sin with Bathsheba was grievous. But only when confronted by Nathan did David fully realize the severity of his sin's consequences. In anguish and remorse, David cried out, "Do not cast me away from Your presence, and do not take Your Holy Spirit from me" (Psalm 51:11 NKJV). What David feared most was a broken relationship with his Father. That is what unrepentant sin does, child. It separates us and becomes a wedge in a relationship that was intended to be close.

In your life today, come to me, confess your sin, and allow me to restore the joy of your salvation. I will renew and refresh your broken spirit. I will uphold and strengthen you so that we will again fellowship together in obedience and love.

Read
Psalm 51:10–12.

Holy Spirit, I confess to you
today my sinfulness and
ask that you create in me a
clean heart.

MARCH 13

I will pour my Spirit upon your offspring, and my blessing on your descendants. They shall spring up among the grass like willows by flowing streams.

—**Isaiah 44:3–4** (ESV)

MY CHOSEN ONES

These were my people, my chosen ones. Out of all the nations of the world, I chose Israel to be my special possession, not because of any merit on their part but because I loved them. Yes, they turned their back on me and worshiped worthless idols. They wandered away from me, but still, they were mine. Despite their stubbornness and their sinfulness, I poured myself out upon them and showered them with blessings. Not only them but their children and their children's children as well.

You too are my chosen one. You are special to me. Even when you wander from me and turn your back on me, I am there, ready to pour out my blessings upon you.

What is it that you need today, child? I am with you. I will make you thrive like a willow by a flowing stream.

Read
Isaiah 44:1–5.

Spirit of God, thank you for the many blessings you have poured out on me.

MARCH 14

The Holy Spirit will come upon you, and the power of the Most High will overshadow you. So the baby to be born will be holy, and he will be called the Son of God.

—**Luke 1:35** (NLT)

MISSION IMPOSSIBLE

Mary's question was an honest one, expected. When Gabriel told her she was to have a child and he was to be called the Son of the Most High, she asked, "How can this happen? I am a virgin" (Luke 1:34 NLT). The angel answered, "The Holy Spirit will come upon you, and the power of the Most High will overshadow you." In one of the greatest mysteries and miracles of human history, a virgin conceived and a son was born who was holy—God incarnate. And he who was born without sin and lived without sin was uniquely qualified to sacrifice his life on a cross for the sins of the world.

Do you doubt that the Most High can intervene in your life and empower you to deal with the struggles you face today? Is there a loved one you believe to be beyond redemption? Remember Mary's question and Gabriel's simple but powerful explanation: "For nothing is impossible with God" (Luke 1:37 NLT).

Read
Luke 1:26 – 38.

Spirit of the Most High, empower me today to overcome, to persevere, and to trust in you.

Jesus answered, "Very truly I tell you, no one can enter the kingdom of God unless they are born of water and the Spirit."

—**John 3:5** (NIV)

REBIRTH

Like Nicodemus, people continue to wonder how to enter the kingdom of God. They look for a formula—a set of rules and regulations to follow that will qualify them to enter heaven, a to-do list they can check off. But Jesus was very clear: no one can enter the kingdom of God unless he or she is born again. It is I who gives new life from heaven. Just as John wrote, "To all who did receive him, to those who believed in his name, he gave the right to become children of God—children born not of natural descent, nor of human decision or a husband's will, but born of God" (John 1:12–13 NIV).

It is the work of the Father, through faith in the Son and the power I provide, that brings about rebirth and the new life that enables one to see the kingdom of God. It is my gift to all who come in faith. Nothing more is required.

You can be reborn, dear one. Nothing is required but for you to trust in the One True God.

Read John 3:1–8.

Spirit, thank you for this gift of new life that enables me to be reborn and enter the kingdom of heaven.

The Spirit of the Lord is upon me, for he has anointed me to bring Good News to the poor. He has sent me to proclaim that captives will be released, that the blind will see.

—Luke 4:18 (NLT)

ANOINTED

As the clouds opened and I descended on Jesus during his baptism, his earthly ministry began. I empowered him to heal the lame, to bring sight to the blind, and to care for the poor. Through each moment of healing and teaching, I guided him as he fulfilled his purpose of proclaiming the gospel.

Dear one, you have also been anointed by the Father. He has chosen you as his child. And just as I was upon the Lord, I am upon you.

The Father's power is at work in you. God has given me to you that others may see his glory. Each time you serve the poor or speak with someone who does not know the Lord, I am working through you. The Father is pleased by your desire to follow after him and tell others about his love for them.

Read Luke 4:14–21.

Lord, may your power work through me today as I share your love with others.

MARCH 17

Brother Saul, the Lord Jesus, who appeared to you on the road, has sent me so that you might regain your sight and be filled with the Holy Spirit.

—Acts 9:17 (NLT)

FEARS AND YOUR FAITH

How it pleased me that our servant Ananias overcame his fears! After I talked to Saul, I wanted to use this chance to grow Ananias's faith as well. When I spoke to Ananias, he was afraid and did not believe that Saul had a change of heart. He was afraid but decided to have faith and trust in my word. Through Ananias's courage, Saul was ministered to and I filled him with my presence.

You sometimes doubt that I know what is best. This saddens me. I know it is part of your sinful nature to have fears. This is not of me. When you do have faith to overcome your fears, this fills me with delight.

When you have faith and go where I tell you to, I will accomplish great things through you just as I did with Ananias. Overcome your fears and have faith.

Read
Acts 9:10–19.

Gracious Spirit, show me where I have suppressed your calling in my life. Give me the faith to overcome my fears.

MARCH 18

*"Did you receive the Holy
Spirit when you believed?"
he asked them. "No," they
replied, "we haven't even
heard that there is a Holy
Spirit."* —**Acts 19:2** (NLT)

PRESENT IN YOU

When Paul traveled to Ephesus and talked to some believers there, he realized they had not yet heard of me. They needed some further teaching so they would understand who I am and be able to receive me. As we worked in the lives of these early believers and laid the foundation for the church, people received me into their lives in a variety of ways. At times, the laying on of hands by my close followers brought me into the lives of new believers. At other times, I came the moment a person repented of his or her sins and believed in the Savior.

The point is not *how* it happens but *that* it happens. The moment you repented of your sins and accepted the sacrifice of Jesus on the cross as payment for your sins, I entered your heart and life. I teach, guide, counsel, comfort, and remind you of the truth.

You don't need to question or wonder about your salvation. If you believe, then I am in you—now and forever.

**Read
Acts 19:1–7.**

*Thank you, Spirit, for
taking up residence in my
life and guiding me daily.*

We do not know what to pray for as we ought, but the Spirit himself intercedes for us with groanings too deep for words.

—**Romans 8:26** (ESV)

I WILL INTERCEDE

I see you there beside your bed, the tears falling silently to the carpet. I know the deep pain in your heart, dear child, and the struggle you have in praying yet again over this situation. I've listened to your pleas. Now you cannot even find any words to pray because you don't know what to say anymore. It all seems helpless, hopeless.

So I pray for you now. I intercede with words that you cannot find. I offer up your requests when you are too weak to do so anymore.

Your prayers are never lost. No request ever goes unnoticed. I know it's difficult to wait so long for an answer that, to you, seems obvious. But trust me, child, we have the best in mind for you. Hang on. Get on your knees, and let me do the praying for you.

Read
Romans 8:23–27.

I sit here silently, Holy Spirit, while you intercede for me in this request.

MARCH 20

On the Lord's Day I was in the Spirit, and I heard behind me a loud voice like a trumpet.

—**Revelation 1:10** (NIV)

WE WIN!

We know how much you want to know what the future holds. When Jesus was on earth, he talked to you about the end times—when he will return to bring all of his followers to be with us forever. He talked about these events, but he did not give a timetable. We know how humans can be: if they knew Jesus wasn't going to return for several years or even their lifetimes, they might be tempted to ignore his teachings altogether.

So even though the end times are not specified, we do want you to understand several things: this earth will not last forever; Jesus is coming back; and, in the end, he will be victorious.

Today is the day to choose whose side you'll be on when Jesus returns. What is your choice?

Read
Revelation 1:9–18.

I choose to follow Jesus, today and every day, and I eagerly await his return for me.

MARCH 21

It was to us that God revealed these things by his Spirit. For his Spirit searches out everything and shows us God's deep secrets.

—1 Corinthians 2:10 (NLT)

THE MYSTERY REVEALED

You cannot begin to understand the glorious future we have prepared for you; in fact, "no eye has seen, no ear has heard, and no mind has imagined what God has prepared for those who love him" (1 Corinthians 2:9 NLT). I have revealed some of this to you, searching out everything and showing God's deep secrets—at least as much as your human mind can comprehend.

I have revealed this to you through God's Word, the Bible. Read there all that we have planned for you. Without me, these words would be pipe dreams. Many who do not have me in their lives cannot believe that such a future is possible, so they turn away in mockery. You, however, have me in your life to help you understand and trust in God's glorious promises. I revealed to you that formerly hidden mystery—salvation in Jesus Christ. The truth of this should give you faith that every other deep secret will one day be revealed as well. Trust me.

Read
1 Corinthians 2.

Thank you in advance for the glorious future you are preparing for me.

The Advocate, the Holy Spirit, whom the Father will send in my name, will teach you all things and will remind you of everything I have said to you.

—John 14:26 (NIV)

TEACHING AND REMINDING

I came from the Father in the name of Jesus in order to teach you all things and remind you of everything Jesus said to the disciples and, by extension, to you in his Word. I continue Jesus' ministry of teaching; I reminded the disciples and Jesus' early followers of everything he taught. The disciples heard the words Jesus spoke, I reminded them of those words, and they wrote them down. This process continues even now as you discover Jesus' words in Scripture.

As you read, study, memorize, and meditate on God's Word, I bring to mind the words you need when you need them. I teach you how to apply the words of Scripture as you walk through life's ups and downs.

Read
John 14:23–26.

Remind me of the words of Scripture when I need them so that I may follow you.

*[The Spirit] will come to you
from the Father and will testify
all about me.*

—John 15:26 (NLT)

WORDS OF POWER

Do you want to be able to share your faith with others, but you don't know how or where to begin? Are you worried that your words will fall flat, that you will be unconvincing?

Relax, child. I came from the Father to testify about the Son. I will guide the words you speak. I will give them power. I will touch the hearts of those who are ready to hear and believe. It's not up to you to convince anyone to believe—you merely need to be ready to share your faith and love for Jesus. As our servant Peter wrote, "Always be prepared to give an answer to everyone who asks you to give the reason for the hope that you have" (1 Peter 3:15 NIV).

Do not be afraid any longer. I will come to you from the Father and will give you the words to say. And the response of the listener is not up to you either; leave it to me. I will plant the seeds where I desire.

Read
John 15:26–27.

*As I share my faith and
my love for Jesus, give my
words power.*

MARCH 24

He will bring me glory by telling you whatever he receives from me.

—**John 16:14** (NLT)

HE IS EVERYTHING

Child, I know how many people boast of their accomplishments in order to appear important, to achieve a moment of glory. They have their reward in the accolades of others. Instead, they should be boasting about all that we have done—the Father, Son, and me.

As the Spirit of truth, I can only speak what is true. I came to speak on behalf of the Son. While on earth, Jesus spoke of the Father and of my coming. Now that I am here, I want to remind you to believe in him. He is the Messiah promised long ago, and he represents the fullness of the glory of God. All authority in heaven and on earth belongs to him. He is everything the prophets promised and more. You can rest the full weight of your trust in him.

Read
John 16:12–16.

Lord, I believe the witness of the Holy Spirit concerning Jesus.

MARCH 25

*If I go not away, the Comforter
will not come unto you; but if I
depart, I will send him unto you.*

—**John 16:7** (KJV)

YOU KNOW THE DIFFERENCE

Sometimes the message I must bring is hard. To those who are unwilling to listen or who balk at the truth, it is unwelcome. Yet that which crumbles must be taken down to its foundation for a new structure to be built.

Consider the image of the Savior: stripped, beaten, and crucified. And then he rose again, crushing death. After his resurrection, Jesus' first thought was of you. He asked me to come as the great Comforter so that you could relax in the knowledge of his sacrifice and step out of the ranks of sin.

By believing that the Son died for you, you begin to understand the difference between what is wicked and what is holy. Through you, others can know this truth as well.

**Read
John 16:7–11.**

*God, I rejoice to know
that my future rests in
Jesus.*

MARCH 26

It is God who establishes us with you in Christ, and has anointed us.

—**2 Corinthians 1:21** (ESV)

SEALED WITH THE SAVIOR

Prophets and kings—I have seen both anointed. And now you, my beloved. Yes, you! You have a priceless gift: my anointing. I rejoice to share with you the indescribable possession of knowing who has formed you, who loves you, and who will be with you every moment of your life.

Can you see what this means? It gives you strength to understand the good news and share it openly and bravely. This blessed anointing manifests differently with each person, but know this: you are wholly set apart and holy through Jesus!

Since I provide the power, you don't have to fumble about in your strength. You are rooted in the Most High, the All-Knowing, the Everlasting. You may access the flowing fount of God's goodness at any time. Drink deeply.

Read
2 Corinthians
1:20–24.

Seal me to your service, Holy One. Anoint and strengthen me.

MARCH 27

He may grant you to be strengthened with power through his Spirit in your inner being, so that Christ may dwell in your hearts through faith.
—Ephesians 3:16–17 (ESV)

THE WORK OF THE SPIRIT

I dwell with you every day. Even on days when you choose to ignore me, I am with you. But when you will take the time to commune with me, I am able to show you the path of righteousness.

I understand that it is not easy to pray every day. Sometimes you even wonder if I'm listening. Rest assured that I am always listening and that I will never leave you. I reside within you, for you have been named by me in heaven, so that I may strengthen you by dwelling in your heart and by giving you the purest love.

It is your choice whether you will allow me to work within you each day. I cannot force you to let me strengthen you. It is by faith that you believe in me, and it is by faith that I make you strong.

Read Ephesians 3:14–17.

Divine Spirit, by faith I invite you into my heart, to strengthen me every day.

The Lord said, My spirit shall not always strive with man, for that he also is flesh: yet his days shall be an hundred and twenty years.

—**Genesis 6:3** (KJV)

MY POWER, YOUR GAIN

I gave humanity a reprieve for over a century before the Flood came. The point was to allow time for anyone to come to repentance. During the wait, I battled the enemy in the world and the sin of people. I restrained evil so that the work of building the ark could be done. Not just the work of the ark, but the work in people's souls.

I still do that today, beloved. When the sun shines and the sky is blue, that means I withheld the storms. When a hurricane hits, I protect lives. When an illness comes, I bring healing.

I know you still see evil in the world. You ask why certain things have been allowed in your life and in others' lives. As bad as things may seem right now, I am still battling the enemy for you. I am still restraining evil from being fully unleashed in order to give you a hope for tomorrow. Turn to me.

Read Genesis 6.

Help me, Holy Spirit, to trust you and believe in your power.

You will be given what to say at that hour, because you are not speaking, but the Spirit of your Father is speaking through you.

—**Matthew 10:19–20** (HCSB)

I SPOKE THROUGH THEM

They were excited. They were nervous. They were scared. Jesus had just finished speaking to the apostles about the trials and beatings they would endure when they went out to preach the gospel. But they would have me with them on their journey. I would speak through them.

I was happy when they stopped worrying about the words they would speak. I loved the confidence they began to have that I would give them the right thing to say at exactly the right time. As they focused on preaching the gospel to the people, I defended the message and spoke of Jesus before even governors and kings.

The more the apostles learned not to be anxious and to trust, the more they were vessels for God's glory—and the more I was able to speak the truth through them to others.

So trust me, child. You too are a vessel for God's glory, and I will speak through you.

**Read
Matthew 10:16–20.**

Holy Spirit, speak through me as you did to the apostles when I am facing persecution.

MARCH 30

The Holy Spirit says: "Today, if you will hear His voice, do not harden your hearts as in the rebellion, in the day of trial in the wilderness."

—Hebrews 3:7–8 (NKJV)

HEAR YE! HEAR YE!

Like the roar of a plane's engine when it starts up, the noise of the world can be deafening. Turn from the noise to me. Cup your ears, calm your heart, and quiet your soul. Hear me today in spite of the noise. I love talking with you. My heart ached when generations ago the Israelites decided not to listen and their hearts became like stones. You can make a different choice.

Keep your heart soft toward me and my work today. It's easy to listen to my voice when I'm speaking words of encouragement that give you hope and strength. It's not as easy other times. My words of truth can be hard to hear, challenging to follow, or even be the opposite of what you want to do. But I really do have your best interests in mind. I want to guide you in righteousness. Walk and talk with me today. Listen to me. I'm here.

Read Hebrews 3:7–11.

Keep me from going astray in my heart, Lord, and help me hear your voice clearly.

MARCH 31

It is the Spirit who gives life; the flesh is no help at all.

—John 6:63 (ESV)

NEW LIFE

Beloved, many strive to hone their flesh in the hope of gaining the perfect body. While taking care of your body is wise, your physical temple will not last forever. It also is not the means by which you can achieve heaven. No matter how much discipline you have, you will never have enough to please God if you don't trust the Son of God.

The flesh of the Son was broken on the cross for you. While many on earth were offended when Jesus spoke of partaking of his flesh and blood, his flesh and blood represented the ultimate sacrifice he would make. Because of that sacrifice, I can give you new life—life that will last throughout eternity. This life is yours for the asking.

Read
John 6:60-65.

Father, thank you for the Spirit's help and the new life he provides.

APRIL

THE FRUIT OF THE SPIRIT: LOVE

APRIL 1

The fruit of the Spirit is love.
—Galatians 5:22 (NKJV)

SAVOR THE FRUIT CALLED LOVE

*L*ove. You have heard the word used in myriad ways. Many claim to love things that are finite: houses, movies, food, and other items. But I am the source of true love. The love I give is so strong it causes one friend to lay down his life for another. Families are bound by it. It is the deep longing a mother feels for the child who never calls or writes; yet she still hopes for his safety, his return. Love is what compels people to help those in need, to reach out to the hurting, to befriend the lonely.

I bestow this blessing upon believers, but beware. Love comes with many attachments—binding cords that connect lives and hearts. A ripple in one person is felt by another. I offer you the rich, tangy, heart-wrenching taste of the fruit called love. Take, savor, and rejoice!

Read
Galatians 5:16–26;
1 John 3:18.

Lord, show me how I might share your lasting, deep love with others.

APRIL 2

This hope will not lead to disappointment. For we know how dearly God loves us, because he has given us the Holy Spirit to fill our hearts with his love.

—**Romans 5:5** (NLT)

LOVE POURED OUT

Your faith in Jesus has justified you before the Father. Think of that—you can stand blameless before the God of the universe because the blood of his Son covered your sins and cleansed you!

Rewarding your faith, God has poured me out into you, filling your heart with the hope of the glory that is to come. No matter what you suffer in this life, I am there to sustain you. I will stand witness to your endurance through life's trials. Your endurance will bring hope because of God's great love for you.

Precious child, God loves you so much he offered his Son as a sacrifice for you. Jesus loves you so much that he willingly died for you. I love you so much that I walk with you today and every day, no matter what the day may bring.

Read Romans 5:1–5.

Jesus, thank you for pouring out your love to me and allowing your Spirit to walk with me daily.

APRIL 3

*I beg you, brethren, through the
Lord Jesus Christ, and through
the love of the Spirit, that you
strive together with me in
prayers to God for me.*

—**Romans 15:30** (NKJV)

WE ARE FAMILY

The love within the family of God is boundless. Paul understood this bond when he asked his brothers in Christ to pray for him. He knew that where three or more are gathered in prayer, I am there carrying their precious requests to the throne of the Almighty.

Love joins believers through prayer. You can demonstrate your love to those within the faith when you promise to pray for them—and keep that promise. When you pray for those outside the faith, you bring me closer to them, allowing me to soften their hearts to the message of the gospel.

Love reaches out and brings others into the family of God. Love never fails.

Read
Romans 15:30–33.

*Lord, thank you for
sending your Spirit to
teach me about your love.*

APRIL 4

Just as you learned it from Epaphras, our beloved fellow bond-servant, who . . . also informed us of your love in the Spirit.

—**Colossians 1:7–8** (NASB)

THE LOVE OF FRIENDS

The people of the church at Colossae were dear to me. They were united together in me, and this became evident to everyone who interacted with them. Their love for God spilled over into their friendship for one another, and their radical hospitality was a bold witness to everyone in need.

Paul wrote to them commending them for their great love for God and friendship for each other even in the midst of trials and suffering. Because they were one in spirit, they withstood the pressures of an unkind world.

Child, seek out those of like mind. Those in whom I dwell will prove themselves as excellent friends. I will lead you to others predestined to work with you in furthering your growth in Christ as well as reaching out for the kingdom of God.

Read Colossians 1:3–14.

Thank you for the gift of friendship, Father. Help me show your love to my friends.

*On the contrary, when he was in
Rome, he searched hard for me
until he found me.*

—2 Timothy 1:17 (NIV)

SEEKING EARNESTLY

Before the universe was spoken into being, I dwelled
in perfect union with the Father and Son. All
relationships are meant to be reflections of the triune God.

When Onesiphorus sought out my faithful servant
Paul, the heavens filled with rejoicing. Here was a man
who placed another's well-being above his own. The Son
spoke of greatest love, and here was a man who listened.

What joy it gives me to see you serve one another!
When you were lost, the Good Shepherd sought you
and brought you back home. Can there be any greater
joy for the King of kings than to see his faithful servants
following his example?

Do not lose heart but pour out yourself in my service.
I will be your Strength and your Provider. Great is your
reward in heaven if you run the course I lay before you.

Read
2 Timothy 1:3–18.

*Lord, don't allow me to
remain indifferent to
those who are perishing.
Stir my heart to action.*

APRIL 6

I am giving you a new commandment: Love each other. Just as I have loved you, you should love each other.

—John 13:34 (NLT)

THE POWER OF LOVE

Look around at the false idols and worthless gods of this world. They promise pleasure and blessing but deliver nothing but weeping and ashes. I alone can satisfy your longings.

The temporary pleasures of this world cannot fulfill you because they cannot love you. I alone know your inner thoughts and truest self, and still I love you. When Christ suffered and died on your behalf, it was so you might know the Lord.

Apart from me, you cannot love those who persecute you. I alone can give you that peace. It is my desire that you would have rest in my arms so that you can share the hope that is within you.

Love is my weapon against the enemy. It breaks the chains of sin and oppression. It was love that drove the Son to sacrifice.

Beloved one, love them all as I have loved you.

Read
John 13:31–38.

God, fill me with your grace. Love the world through me.

APRIL 7

Love must be sincere. Hate what is evil; cling to what is good.

—**Romans 12:9** (NIV)

LOVING THE UNLOVELY

Learning to love, to really love others in the way that I intend for you to love them, is one of the most important things you will ever do. I know this task is difficult; asking you to love everyone means loving those who are self-centered and have darkness in their hearts. I can help you.

The most important thing is to be sincere. If you profess to have love in your heart for someone but secretly do not, your efforts will be of no worth to them or to yourself. Until you see others as I see them, you will never love them.

Remember this: although I am not blind to the sins of my creations, I see their virtues too. Allow me to show you how to see what is lovely inside the unlovely people. When you learn to see the good in them, you will be able to love them with the sincerity of my love.

Read
Romans 12.

Show me what is good and lovely in the people I meet today.

Love your neighbor as yourself.

—**Romans 13:9** (NIV)

LOVE DOES NO HARM

In 1 Peter 4:8, it says, "Love covers over a multitude of sins" (NIV). But love also *keeps* you from a multitude of sins. This is why love is the greatest of the gifts from God. Loving someone as you love yourself means that you take joy in their joy and feel empathy with their sorrows. You avoid actions you know will hurt them because you can imagine what that hurt would feel like yourself, and you do not begrudge them their joy because you wish happiness for them. When you love others this way, it pleases me.

I know it is not easy for you to love everyone this way. If it was, how would that glorify God? Choose to show love for these people anyway. Choose to make decisions that will benefit them and not hurt them, that will bring them joy and not sorrow. I will help you with this if you let me. I will show you how to love them if you ask me.

Read
Romans 13.

Please show me how to love my neighbors as myself.

If I speak with the tongues of men and of angels, but do not have love, I have become a noisy gong or a clanging cymbal.

—1 Corinthians 13:1 (NASB)

INFUSED WITH LOVE

Words fill many moments of your day—talking to a friend, chatting with a neighbor, conversing with a coworker. Perhaps today you spoke beautiful words, but you felt like they were nothing more than noise. Something was missing—a warmth, a compassion, a joy.

Child, my love fills in that missing piece. Infuse your words today with the harmony of my love—with notes of patience, kindness, humility, steadfastness, forgiveness, perseverance, endurance, hopefulness, and rejoicing; chords mixing and matching to create just the right score for whomever you meet today.

That's why I'm here with you today—to give you my love. It's a love that goes beyond feelings to an act of the will to bless others.

Are you ready? I am. Let me help you speak to others today in ways that are as exquisite as the cuts on a diamond and as delicate as a spring flower—all because of my love.

Read
1 Corinthians 13.

Holy Spirit, help my words to be infused with love and not a noisy gong or clanging cymbal.

For you were called to
freedom, brothers. Only do
not use your freedom as an
opportunity for the flesh, but
through love serve one another.
—**Galatians 5:13** (ESV)

SERVING IN LOVE

Child, what is on your to-do list today? What are those matters that are pressing upon you? What is keeping you up at night? Is it getting a promotion? Being successful? Finding a relationship that you believe will bring you true fulfillment? Whatever earthly pursuits you are running after, remember that you have been called to a life of freedom—freedom, though, not to pursue your own agenda but the freedom to serve one another in love.

Remember, as Paul told the church in Galatia: you have been saved not by deeds but through faith, and this not through your own efforts but by grace. Loving others through acts of service is an expression of that faith and the proper response to grace.

Who can you serve today? How can you share love with others by helping them, encouraging them? That's a to-do list that glorifies me.

**Read
Galatians 5.**

*Spirit of love, show me who
I can serve today in love.*

APRIL 11

For the entire law is fulfilled in one statement: Love your neighbor as yourself.

—**Galatians 5:14** (HCSB)

THE WAY TO LOVE

As Jesus and Moses knew, the sum of all the law can be summed up in one command: "Love your neighbor as yourself." You might wonder if that command seems selfish or wrong. Yet who among you doesn't take care of yourself to the best of your ability? Do you not monitor your health and well-being—making sure you have food to eat, clothes to wear, a roof over your head, and other basic needs?

In the same way, show that love for self to others around you. Who is in need of food, clothing, or shelter? How can you love those around you by providing for their needs? By actively working to see that the needs of others are met, you are loving others as yourself. And that, child, is the true way to love.

**Read
Galatians 5:14–15.**

Just as I care for my basic needs, Spirit, show me how to care for the needs of others.

Do not take revenge or bear a grudge against members of your community, but love your neighbor as yourself; I am Yahweh.

—**Leviticus 19:18** (HCSB)

LOVE YOUR NEIGHBOR AS YOURSELF

I t is I, the Spirit of the Lord, who arouses compassion to replace revenge. It is I who instills peace when anger arises. It is I who substitutes calm for anxiety, logic for brashness, and patience for aggression. If you wish to serve the Almighty, you must begin by controlling your own passions and inclinations toward bearing a grudge or desiring revenge. When you yield to my guidance, love can abound, forgiveness can reign, and kindness can prevail.

The Scriptures proclaim, "The tongue of the righteous is choice silver; the heart of the wicked is worth little" (Proverbs 10:20 NKJV). I will aid your words in being choice silver to your neighbor. I will help you let go of the hurt.

Read
Leviticus 19:15–18.

You have taught me, wise Spirit, that as I love my neighbor, I refresh my soul.

APRIL 13

*The LORD is slow to anger
and filled with unfailing love,
forgiving every kind of sin and
rebellion.*

—**Numbers 14:18** (NLT)

HIS FAITHFUL LOVE

As you have walked with Jesus, I have seen your struggles and pain. I have been with you during every rejection, every mistake, and every tear. Sadly, these are the effects of sin. The sins of your grandparents and parents still affect you.

Dear one, I hold your future in my hands. If you ask for forgiveness, I am rich in faithful love. Do not be afraid to ask me for forgiveness or love, for I have both in abundance. Don't be afraid to love, for that is a characteristic of me. Love can influence the generations. Let my love redeem you.

**Read
Numbers 14:15–20.**

*Thank you for your
faithful love, Father.
Forgive me and let me
love others like you
love me.*

APRIL 14

You shall love the LORD your God with all your heart, with all your soul, and with all your strength.

—**Deuteronomy 6:5** (NKJV)

LOVE GOD

When Moses went to the people of Israel with the Ten Commandments, he told them the greatest commandment was to love God with their entire being.

That is the most important thing you can do: love God with all you are. To truly love him means to love God with all your heart, soul, and strength. By this, you love his Word and his creations. I know at times it is hard to love like this. Your plans and your busy life get in the way. But believe me when I say that you were created to give that kind of love.

I am here to help you understand the depth of love the Father, the Son, and I have for you. Understanding our love helps you learn how to love us better.

Read
Deuteronomy
6:1–9.

Spirit, help me love God with everything I have today.

Give thanks to the LORD, for he is good! His faithful love endures forever.

—**1 Chronicles 16:34** (NLT)

ENDURING LOVE

I have always been with the Father, and I have never experienced an end to his love.

Not once.

When the Father flooded the earth, when the Israelites destroyed the Canaanites, when a mother of four died of cancer, and even when a man left his family for a bottle, the Father's love endured. You see, the Father *is* love and is incapable of anything else. If a woman rejects him, the Father continues to pursue her. When a man's mind is shrouded by sin, the Father's love uncovers it.

The Father adores you, and that is why he sacrificed his Son to save you. Rejoice and do not keep this knowledge to yourself. Care for others at all times. For the Father always cares for you. Regard those around you in the same way. Express a love to them that endures forever.

**Read
1 Chronicles 16:7–36.**

Help me to have an enduring love, so I can care for others as you do.

Love the LORD, all you his saints! The LORD preserves the faithful but abundantly repays the one who acts in pride.

—**Psalm 31:23** (ESV)

THE FRUIT OF THE SPIRIT IS LOVE

There are many things in this world to distract you: movies, books, music, television, the Internet. I want you to enjoy these things, of course, but the enemy can use them to turn your heart from me.

If you say you love me, then pray to me. Talk with me. Read the words I have given you in Scripture. Love your neighbor, your spouse, your siblings, your parents. All these things show my love to others and my love to you. I will keep you safe within my arms when the storms come, because you love me and I love you.

You are my saints, my children, my ambassadors. The world can often be a cold place, but the world cannot deny love, no matter how hard it tries. So love me as I love you, and love people as I love people.

Read Psalm 31.

Loving others and loving you is difficult, Holy Spirit. Help me to love you, and help me to love others.

APRIL 17

Hate evil, love good; maintain justice in the courts. Perhaps the LORD *God Almighty will have mercy on the remnant of Joseph.*

—**Amos 5:15** (NIV)

MY LOVE IS FIERCE

Do you understand how I love? I burn with love for you, and I despise any sin that brings you to harm.

When you walk with me, I dance with joy like a fire. But just as my love is fierce, my hate is fierce. And I hate it when you hurt yourself. You sometimes let sin get in the way of my love for you. Love me and my path so that you may fully experience my love. Despise that which is evil so that we may be together.

I know the great evil and the great good in you, so I am gracious to you. Try to live for me and experience my love. My love overcomes the darkness and will bring you into the light.

Read
Amos 5:5–15.

Help me rejoice in the good the Spirit has shown me and avoid the bad that can hurt me.

APRIL 18

He has shown you, O mortal, what is good. And what does the LORD require of you? To act justly and to love mercy and to walk humbly with your God. —Micah 6:8 (NIV)

BACK TO BASICS

I have been opening the eyes of the faithful for thousands of years. I have shown kings and paupers, queens and servants, the very same thing. What heaven requires of those who live on earth hasn't changed. And neither has my quiet way of making it clear to you.

It is my joy to reveal to those who long for godliness what it is that matters most in life. Beloved, you know what I have shown you. Walking humbly with the Father is the key. When you heed my voice and walk with God, you have an overwhelming desire to act with fairness. Walking with your eyes focused on the Father's agenda also results in being merciful. You love to show mercy to those who have made mistakes or been the victims of others' abuse. And today you have a chance to walk with God into the lives of those who need him the most. I will guide you if you let me.

Read
Micah 6:6–8.

Today I will act fairly and show mercy as I humbly walk with you.

This is what the LORD of
Heaven's Armies says: Judge
fairly, and show mercy and
kindness to one another.

—**Zechariah 7:9** (NLT)

PLAYING FAIR

Being fair. Showing mercy. Dispensing kindness. It's just my way. That's how the Father, Son, and I treat each other. It's our nature. And that is the way we have created you to be as well. Oh yes, I know. You can come up with endless reasons to get even or to pull away from someone in an attempt to prove your point or to gain the upper hand. But what is to be gained by that strategy long-term?

What I am asking of you is the very ability I am giving to you. Work fair. Play fair. Be fair in all your dealings with others today. To the degree you have received mercy and kindness from heaven, follow suit. I will nudge you when you begin to make excuses. I will applaud you when you act like me.

**Read
Zechariah 7:8–12.**

With your help I will resist the temptation to get even or assert my way.

APRIL 20

*If you love those who love you,
what reward will you get?
Are not even the tax collectors
doing that?*

—**Matthew 5:46** (NIV)

LOVE THE UNLOVABLE

My dear one, if you love those who love you, is that
not your reward? Loving your enemy is what is
truly difficult. If you treat your enemies with kindness and
pray for those who persecute you, this will bring heavenly
rewards for you.

I choose to allow good things to happen to the good
and the bad, the righteous and the unrighteous. I do this
to see how you will react—whether you will curse or bless.
When you act righteously in bad times as well as good,
this pleases me. However, if you only act righteously in
the good times and love those who love you, there will be
no reward.

Love those who hate you. This is my way. No one
has ever deserved the love I have given them. Loving the
unlovable is difficult, but it's what I do, so I want you to
do the same.

Read
Matthew 5:43–46.

*Holy Spirit, help me to see
the good in those I want to
hate. Help me to see with
your eyes.*

APRIL 21

*Neither of them had the money
to pay him back, so he forgave
the debts of both. Now which of
them will love him more?*

—**Luke 7:42** (NIV)

LOVE FORGIVES

When Jesus told the Pharisee Simon the parable about the two debtors who were forgiven, Simon answered correctly when he said that the one whose debt was the largest was the one who loved most. The Son told how the woman who anointed his feet loved him more because she had been forgiven of more sins.

There is no greater love than the Father's love. Indeed, he sent his Son to die so that he could forgive the sins of those who come to him through the Son. The Father is just. But he also loves. It is through his love for you that he forgives you. It is through his love that the Son forgave the sins of the woman at his feet.

Beloved, I can help you show the love of the Father to others through the forgiveness you offer. Love forgives.

**Read
Luke 7:36–50.**

*Help me to love as Christ
loved and forgive as the
Father has forgiven.*

If you love me, you will keep my commandments.

—John 14:15 (ESV)

OBEY ME

In the Upper Room Jesus shared a meal with his disciples. During the meal he exhorted them to keep his commandments. He promised he would not leave them without help in this task. He would send me to them and to you. The world cannot receive me, because it doesn't know me. But you love the Son and, through him, you know me.

You can sense my presence as you keep the Son's commandments. I go with you as you walk through each step of your day seeking to obey. I see the struggle when you confront your own sinfulness, when old habits rear their ugly heads, when temptation attacks. I offer you my strength. I give you my support. I cheer you on when you succeed because I know you want to obey. You want to obey because you love us.

This is not an impossible task, dear child. Just take one step at a time and look to me. I will help you.

Read
John 14:15–21.

Spirit, help me to keep your commandments and know you as my Comforter.

Anyone who loves me will obey my teaching. My Father will love them, and we will come to them and make our home with them.

—John 14:23 (NIV)

YOU HAVE A HOME

I know the world is a hard place. I know there have been times when you've made mistakes or tried to go your own way. Even in those moments, in those trials, I am with you. At all times, my hand has guided you along the way. And no matter how many times you disobey, my love for you will not go away. I will always wait for you and you will *always* have a home with me.

The Father and the Son sent me to be with you, forever. I am here to lead you, to teach you, and to remind you of the Father's great love for you. It's not always easy to follow my lead, but that is how others will see me at work in you.

Dear one, please follow my guidance, for I know what is best for you and I know how much you love me.

Read John 14:15–25.

Please help me follow your lead, even when it's hard, today and each day.

Greater love has no one than this, that someone lay down his life for his friends.

—**John 15:13** (ESV)

A PERFECT LOVE STORY

You are living the greatest love story ever written. But this love story is different. God—the all-knowing Creator of the universe—loves you. His love for you is not like human love. It never changes or goes away. The Father's love for you is perfect.

God loves you so much that he sent his only Son to die in your place. And he sent me as a reminder of his great love for you. As you remain in me, you will know his love; for the Father, the Son, and I are one.

Dear child, the Father longs for you to love him in the same way. It brings him great pleasure when you put him first in your life. Today, beloved, choose to love your heavenly Father the way he loves you. For when you love the Father, others will know his love—because God is love.

Read John 15:9–17.

Thank you for loving me perfectly. Help me love you and put you first in my life.

APRIL 25

*But God demonstrates His own
love toward us, in that while we
were still sinners, Christ died
for us.*

—**Romans 5:8** (NKJV)

LOVE DIED FOR US

Firefighters, police officers, and soldiers are considered
heroes because they risk their lives to save others.
It might be considered part of their job, but it also is a
work of love and sacrifice. A person might not hesitate to
give his or her life for a friend. But would someone risk
death for a sworn enemy? Would people put themselves in
danger to bring back one wretched person who didn't love
them?

Praise God that he is above man's ways. Christ's
sacrifice was not one of duty or even friendship. It was a
sacrifice of love. All who were unsaved were enemies of
God, yet he died to bring everyone back—everyone!

I want you to have the joy of knowing that God loves
you every day for the rest of your life. I want you to give
praise in light of this wondrous love. Through Christ, you
have been reconciled. What a loving sacrifice!

**Read
Romans 5:5–11.**

*Dear Father, thank you
for your love. Let me
rejoice in your wondrous
sacrifice all my days.*

APRIL 26

*Obey my commandments
that I command you today, to
love the LORD your God, and
to serve him with all your
heart and with all your soul.*

—**Deuteronomy 11:13** (ESV)

LOVE WITHOUT HYPOCRISY

Child, love is the beginning and the end of obedience.
When genuine love is practiced, every commandment
is obeyed. To love is to honor another above yourself
and to desire goodness for the object of your affection.
Love will not steal, love will not lie, love will not desire
something that belongs to another. Genuine love does not
gossip about a brother. It does not think evil things about
a neighbor. It does not wish for harm or embarrassment to
retaliate for a wrong.

I hear the word *love* bantered about much too often
in this world. How it saddens me to hear this word spoken
insincerely among God's children. Too often a man will
say he loves his brother and then complain to a neighbor
about something his brother has done. Real love, dear one,
must be without such hypocrisy. I am pleased when you
sincerely love others.

**Read
Deuteronomy
11:8–15.**

*Spirit, please fill my heart
today with your genuine
love. Amen.*

APRIL 27

Love does no wrong to a neighbor; therefore love is the fulfillment of the law.

—**Romans 13:10** (NASB)

LOVE IN MOTION

Jesus' loving sacrifice was the final fulfillment of the law. Jesus, the embodiment of love, was beaten by those to whom he had given life and who were determined to take away his. Yet he willingly gave up his life. For you.

Love moves, lifts, plans. Love offers more than lip service; it genuinely cares for others. I have empowered that kind of love enacted by believers in ways little and large. To those who listen when they have other things to do. To those who care enough to bring a meal to a widow, pay a bill for someone in need, or babysit for a tired parent. I provide the power and the grace to put love in motion.

Will you let me love through you today?

Read
Romans 13:8–10.

Heavenly Father, show me those who need you. Help me show your love to them.

God is so rich in mercy, and
he loved us so much.

—**Ephesians 2:4** (NLT)

LOVE AND MERCY

Oh, dear child, a thousand years is not long enough for me to sing of my love for you. I know your finite mind. You need tangible examples to help you understand that love. Consider when a mother first sees her baby or when a father looks with pride on his son's accomplishments. Consider a friend offering forgiveness to one who has betrayed her. All are aspects of love.

I breathed life into Adam. Yet in that moment, I also knew what Adam would do to grieve me and what had to be done to save him. That's why the Son was sent—out of love and mercy. You can always count on the love and mercy of God. Drink in the mercies you have been given as a child of God.

Read
Ephesians 2:13–22.

Thank you for this new
citizenship. May I never
forget your mercy.

*Speaking the truth in love, we
are to grow up in all aspects into
Him who is the head.*

—**Ephesians 4:15** (NASB)

SPEAK TRUTH IN LOVE

Beloved, how beautiful a timely word can be. Yet how quickly harmful words fly like missiles out of the mouths of many people, some of whom claim to speak for me. And like missiles, these words detonate upon impact. Such injurious words linger in the mind long afterward.

I can give you power to speak truth. I also can give you the love that enables you to speak in a way that builds up rather than tears down.

Remember the way that the Savior walked while on earth. He modeled the grace and firmness inherent in speaking the truth in love. I can help you imitate him.

**Read
Ephesians 4:15–16.**

*Lord, grant me the
humility and the
overwhelming love to
speak truth to others.*

Above all, keep loving one another earnestly, since love covers a multitude of sins.

—1 Peter 4:8 (ESV)

CHOOSING TO LOVE

It's a new day. A chance to love others again. I know it can be hard to forgive yesterday's misspoken word, unfortunate mistake, careless expression, or grievous deed—especially when it comes from a brother or sister in Christ. But my love makes it possible to do what seems impossible.

Give the pain of yesterday to me, child. You don't have to bear it alone. Let me intercede for you with the Father. Reflect on my love instead of the pain.

Remember what I've given you? I've shown the way when you've faltered. I've extended grace in your mistakes. I've forgiven you when you've sinned. Take my love. Lean into it. Let it guide you one step at a time. And let it strengthen your resolve. Then, choose to give my love away. Love others today with my love—fervently, earnestly, and abundantly.

Read
1 Peter 4:7–11.

Holy Spirit, help me to show the fruit of your love in my life by loving others with your love.

MAY

THE FRUIT OF THE SPIRIT: JOY

MAY 1

The fruit of the Spirit is . . . joy.

—**Galatians 5:22** (KJV)

SAVOR THE FRUIT CALLED JOY

Child, I hear some say that all they want out of life is happiness. They think it can be purchased or gained by simply putting their minds to it. But "being happy" and wearing a pasted-on smile do not indicate actual joy.

To have an opportunity to savor my fruit called joy first means having a relationship with the Savior and allowing me to fill you to the brim.

Believers possessing my precious gift find joy abounding in unexpected places: in a dank prison cell or during a season of defeat and anguish. Such challenges offer surprising glimpses of true joy.

Whatever circumstances you are facing today, look for the fruit of joy I am offering you, even in unexpected places.

**Read
Psalm 68:3;
Galatians 5:16–26.**

Lord, let me experience the joy of your salvation and you, the fount of all joy.

MAY 2

All the people came up after him, and the people piped with pipes, and rejoi_ _d with great joy, so that the earth rent with the sound of them.

—1 Kings 1:40 (KJV)

EARTH-SHATTERING JOY

The joy I provide was not meant to be quiet, contained, or controlled. It is boundless indeed.

You've heard of singers who can shatter a crystal goblet when they sing a high note. In the time of King David, the rejoicing of many actually split the earth. God's prophet, Nathan, assisted in assuring that David's son, Solomon, would succeed David as king of Israel. When someone else attempted to usurp the throne, David put things right. As a result, the people celebrated with shouts and dances of joy with enough magnitude to produce an earthquake.

Solomon requested, and was granted, wisdom from God (1 Kings 3:9–12). He is known as the wisest king in history—no wonder the people he ruled were so happy!

So, pray. When I answer, don't hold your joy inside; let it out for everyone to hear. Celebrate my goodness! Split the earth with your joy!

Read
1 Kings 1:28–40.

Your Spirit brings me joy, Lord. You have blessed me, and I cannot contain my joy.

MAY 3

I have spoken these things to you so that My joy may be in you and your joy may be complete.

—**John 15:11** (HCSB)

THE FRUIT OF JOY IN THE VINE

Jesus has promised you an abundance of joy! My presence in you provides that abundance.

As he walked in the vineyard with his disciples, Jesus knew the time to lay down his life had drawn near. His late-night stroll in the garden with his most beloved friends provided him the opportunity to share an important parting message: if you remain in him and bear the fruit of a faithful life, your joy will overflow.

Remember that joy is not the same as happiness. Happiness comes and goes with circumstances; joy is a deep-seated condition of the heart anchored in the Author of your faith. Joy comes from being a fruit-bearing branch that draws its nourishment from the Vine.

Jesus is the source of true joy. Remain in him today and every day, dear one, so that your joy may be complete.

Read John 15:1–11.

Jesus, you are my vine. Help me to bear good fruit and to reap an abundance of joy.

MAY 4

May the God of hope fill you with all joy and peace in believing, so that by the power of the Holy Spirit you may abound in hope.

—**Romans 15:13** (ESV)

FILLED WITH JOY . . . AND MORE!

Hope, joy, and peace go hand in hand. Hope is the ability to look forward to the future that God has in store for you, confident that he who began a good work in you will be faithful to complete it (Philippians 1:6). Joy is the feeling of great delight, knowing that the Father has prepared a place for you that no one can steal or destroy. Peace comes from the harmony you have with your Creator and the security of your salvation.

By my power within you, you are filled with all three facets of this precious gem. And like a polished, perfectly cut diamond, your belief sparkles for all to see. People are drawn by the beauty of your hope, joy, and peace made brilliant by the glory of God in your life.

You are more precious than you realize, child. Rejoice in the power and hope of your salvation.

Read Romans 15:8–13.

I rejoice in you, my Savior and my Redeemer!

Rejoice in the Lord always;
again I will say, rejoice.

—**Philippians 4:4** (ESV)

ALWAYS REJOICE

How I love to hear you rejoicing in me! There are days when your joy overflows and bubbles forth like an artesian mountain spring, refreshing everyone who comes into contact with you. But there are days when you find rejoicing to be a difficult task to master.

I am with you in every circumstance—in your joys and in your sorrows. When you dance, I dance with you. When you mourn, I comfort you. After all, many refer to me as the Comforter.

Always rejoicing doesn't mean you have to fake a smile on the worst of days. Always rejoicing means praising the Lord for the good times and thanking the Lord that he sent me to comfort you during the bad times. It means laying your worries in my hands and trusting that God is in control.

So, dear one, no matter what today holds, rejoice. Again I say it: rejoice!

**Read
Philippians 4:4–9.**

I rejoice in you, O Lord!
Thank you for rejoicing
with me and comforting me.

You became imitators of us and of the Lord, for you received the word in much affliction, with the joy of the Holy Spirit.

—**1 Thessalonians 1:6** (ESV)

JOY: A WAY OF LIFE

I've said it to you before, that happiness and joy are not one and the same. Happiness is fleeting, a mood dictated by events. Joy is a way of life.

Joy does not depend upon circumstances. Real joy comes from knowing Jesus as your Savior and having my presence residing within your heart. Your mood may change due to pain, heartbreak, and trials, but the deep-down joy in being a child of God will never leave you.

Jesus said it best: "I will never leave you nor forsake you" (Hebrews 13:5 ESV). This truth can bring inexpressible, unfathomable elation to your heart! The God of the universe sent me to dwell in you so you would never have to be alone.

Weeping may last for a night, but the joy that comes from your Savior will sustain you from now until you see the Source of all joy face-to-face.

**Read
1 Thessalonians 1.**

My Savior, thank you for being the source of my joy.

Rejoice always.

—1 Thessalonians 5:16
(NASB)

RECIPE FOR JOY

What endless joy belongs to you, child of God! In times of plenty, I am with you, filling you with praise for the good things you have received. And in times of trial, I give you the strength to praise anyway.

What victory can death or pain hold over you? In the pleasant times, I draw your gaze to the throne of God. In the trials, consider yourself blessed to suffer for the glory of my name. Eternally, I shelter you in my wings and refresh your spirit.

Rejoice! Nothing can pluck you out of my hand. I will never leave you, and my strength will never fade. That is a blessing greater than any other. Aside from my love, every good thing is ashes.

And I love you, dear one. I will always be with you. Rejoice!

Read
1 Thessalonians
5:12–28.

Lord, I celebrate my identity as your child.

MAY 8

Though you have not seen him, you love him. Though you do not now see him, you believe in him and rejoice with joy that is inexpressible and filled with glory.

—1 Peter 1:8 (ESV)

CLINGING TO THE UNSEEN

Since the day you were born, I have been there. I have whispered to your soul the truth of the Son, in order that you might know God.

For millennia, the enemy has fought to kill the hope and joy of Christ's revelation, but it shall not happen! When my servants endured suffering for the sake of the gospel, I gave them the joy that comes only from me. Child, cling to the voice of truth, even in the face of persecution and hardship. In all things you have the authority of God, for you bear my name. Let this be more precious to you than all the riches of this world. The sovereign God calls you by name.

Though the darkness prowls about, the Lord your God is your Protector. You will not fall victim to the evil one, for I will crush him beneath your feet. Celebrate, for I am faithful.

Read
1 Peter 1:1–9.

God, help me sense your presence always. When I feel distant from you, remind me of your love.

MAY 9

*Many sacrifices were offered
on that joyous day, for God
had given the people cause for
great joy.*

—**Nehemiah 12:43** (NLT)

GOD GIVES GREAT JOY

You were created to fellowship with God. And so it is that God and mankind can share laughter, joy, celebration, and happiness. I gave great joy to Nehemiah when the walls of Jerusalem were rebuilt. And David gleefully proclaimed, "Let all who take refuge in you rejoice; let them sing joyful praises forever. Spread your protection over them, that all who love your name may be filled with joy" (Psalm 5:11 NLT).

I, the Spirit, will open your heart to delight. I will nourish your soul with contentment. I will imbue your mind with amazement. I will give a dance to your feet and a song to your lips. Mutual rejoicing is a holy bonding of the Creator with his created ones. My blessing comes by instilling a joyous nature in all of God's children. Rejoice, and again I say, rejoice!

Read
Nehemiah 12:40–47.

*Each day I celebrate the joy
of being loved by God.*

MAY 10

*Lo, God will not reject a man of
integrity, nor will He support the
evildoers. He will yet fill your
mouth with laughter and your
lips with shouting.*

—Job 8:20–21 (NASB)

INTEGRITY

Acceptance matters. From the time you were a child,
you wanted to feel accepted by others. That hasn't
changed now that you are older. Nobody likes being
rejected; it goes against the way you were designed. You
were made to be transparent and consistent in all your
ways.

Beloved, I will not reject you when you choose to
be a person of integrity. In fact, when you do what you
say and put feet to your faith, it shows. Your whole body
responds in a positive way. Integrity frees me to fill your
heart with happiness and your mouth with laughter. Your
eyes will twinkle with joy as you lift your arms toward
heaven in worship.

But remember, integrity is a choice. Every day you
must decide to embrace consistency and honesty. I will
help you.

Read
Job 8:19–22.

*Help me feel your smile
as I walk my talk today.*

MAY 11

God has delivered me from going down to the pit, and I shall live to enjoy the light of life.

—**Job 33:28** (NIV)

MERCY AND GRACE

Mercy and grace. They are nearly identical twins. Someone has said that mercy is not getting the awful consequences that you deserve and grace is being given something wonderful that you don't deserve. When it comes to the Father, you are the recipient of his abundant mercy and grace. It is my great joy to communicate that truth to you, beloved. For you, in fact, are loved! I am the one who reminds you that you are forgiven. I am the one who opens your eyes as you read Scripture to identify with the unmitigated joy that Job describes.

Don't let anyone convince you otherwise. There is nothing you could ever do (be it wonderful or horrific) that would cause you to be outside of my love or earn more of my love than you have right this very moment. And it's my job to keep you believing that.

Will you let me?

Read Job 33:26–28.

To the degree I have been loved by you, God, I will aim to love you and love others today.

You will show me the way of life, granting me the joy of your presence and the pleasures of living with you forever.

—Psalm 16:11 (NLT)

TRUE JOY

Are you searching for happiness today, child? Do you want to know the true source of joy? King David discovered it thousands of years ago. Despite a life that was often filled with heartaches and disappointment, failure and sin, David was able to rejoice and live joyfully because he knew I was always with him. His joy was not dependent on his circumstances but on my presence alone. Consider his words: "I know the LORD is always with me. I will not be shaken, for he is right beside me. No wonder my heart is glad, and I rejoice" (Psalm 16:8–9 NLT).

No wonder, indeed. If you are looking for happiness today, don't look to your current circumstances or your bank account, or even your relationships with others. Know that I am with you always, and that in my presence, you will find the source of true joy.

Read Psalm 16.

Holy Spirit, help me to look beyond my circumstances and live today in the joy of your presence.

MAY 13

*I have no greater joy than
this: to hear that my children
are walking in the truth.*

—3 John 4 (HCSB)

WALK IN TRUTH

The Father longs to see you living the best life that he has for you. He wants you to experience the true joy that comes from walking in his ways. Yet it is only when you live your life according to the truths in his Word that you can have this life, because true joy cannot be found apart from God.

True joy is the joy of knowing who you are in Christ, understanding that you are loved by the Father and surrounded by my presence. This joy comes from inside you and does not depend on your circumstances. You forfeit this joy when you do not heed my voice telling you how to live according to the Word.

It is my job to be with you and to guide you into all truth. When you walk with me, you walk in truth, and this pleases the Father.

**Read
3 John.**

*Help me to experience the
joy that comes from walking
in the truth.*

MAY 14

Rejoice insofar as you share Christ's sufferings, that you may also rejoice and be glad when his glory is revealed.

—1 Peter 4:13 (ESV)

JOY WILL FOLLOW SUFFERING

According to the world, choosing to follow Christ is an unpopular decision. It was unpopular in the beginning and it is still unpopular now. It will never be popular, but it will always be right.

Being a follower of Christ means that there will be times throughout your life when people may ridicule you, avoid you, and even hate you for what you believe. They may deride you openly or mock you behind your back. Do not worry, although this causes you pain in the moment, for the time will come when your faith will be justified and all your suffering rewarded.

I am here to help you, to comfort you in the midst of these trials, and to remind you of the promises in the Word of God. Stand strong despite the cruel words and hurtful actions of others. Endure to the end, and you will have cause to be joyful on that glorious day of Christ's return.

Read
1 Peter 4:12–19.

Remind me to rejoice in the persecutions I endure, knowing the joy that awaits me.

MAY 15

Count it all joy, my brothers,
when you meet trials of
various kinds.

—James 1:2 (ESV)

JOY IN YOUR TROUBLES

Beloved, I know you sometimes doubt that joy
can be gained when you encounter difficulties.
Not many would agree that there is joy in heartache,
disappointments, or failure. No one would expect you to
rejoice when you have lost your job or your spouse has
walked away, or to celebrate when the test results come
back and your doctor says, "You have cancer."

But child, there *can* be joy in the face of hardships.
Joy is not about pretending to be happy or acting as if
there is nothing wrong; it is a deeper realization that
this particular hardship is an opportunity to grow in
faith. Through my fruit, I will fill you with the joy of
my presence, of the knowledge that I will enable you to
persevere, and of the certainty that, in the end, you will
overcome and be strengthened because of what you have
endured.

When you face a difficulty, count it all joy.

Read
James 1.

Fill me with your joy, Lord,
that I might be able to
persevere and overcome.

MAY 16

Fixing our eyes on Jesus, the author and perfecter of faith, who for the joy set before Him endured the cross, despising the shame, and has sat down at the right hand of the throne of God.

—Hebrews 12:2 (NASB)

FOCUS ON HIM

The last few days have been stressful, haven't they, child? Indeed, you are so bogged down with work and other commitments that it's hard to keep a genuine smile on your face. You wish to do everything on your own, but you can't. You've forgotten to give everything to me, and because of that, you are tired and cannot see the joy in what you are doing.

I have surrounded you with people who will help you focus on me and not on your commitments. When you're focused on me, the commitments don't seem so many or so large. With the joy I give you, everything you do is for my glory, and it all proclaims my love and joy to those who see you.

So don't worry, and don't stress. Just surrender to me everything that has kept you busy lately. I will help you take care of it and give you the joy that comes from doing things in my name.

Read
Hebrews 12:1–2.

Holy Spirit, it's hard to find joy when I'm stressed. I surrender everything to you.

MAY 17

*Your words became to me
a joy and the delight of my
heart, for I am called by your
name, O LORD, God of hosts.*

—**Jeremiah 15:16** (ESV)

WORDS OF JOY

Beloved, I love our times together. I love when you
tell me about your joys, fears, and plans. I grieve
when distractions worm into my time with you. Sleep
and work are important, but my time with you is crucial
to your spiritual well-being. How can you serve me when
your soul is impoverished?

Jeremiah, known as "the weeping prophet," faced
many hardships. However, he found joy in my words,
consuming them for sustenance. I want to give you the
same joy I gave Jeremiah.

Our Word is like the air you breathe: you cannot
live without it. Read it; study it as though your every
heartbeat and breath depends on it. Only then can you
discover the joy I offer.

Read
Jeremiah 15:16–19.

*Speak to my heart through
your words, O God, and give
me your joy.*

MAY 18

The LORD your God is with you,
the Mighty Warrior who saves.
He will take great delight in
you; in his love he will no longer
rebuke you, but will rejoice over
you with singing.

—**Zephaniah 3:17** (NIV)

JOY IN MY PRESENCE

I cannot express the joy I felt when you were first saved, dear one. How delightful it is to know that you will be with me forever! I sought you when you were lost. I freed you from your entanglement. You have accepted the gift of salvation through the sacrifice of Jesus, and I have thrown your sins as far away from me as the east is from the west. Now, nothing can separate you from my love.

What is there now to rob you of contentment? What greater joy is there, child, than the knowledge that you are mine? There is no greater happiness for me than looking upon the redeemed. You shall have this joy on earth as you shall also have an inheritance in the kingdom. I rejoiced the day you were claimed, and together we will celebrate the victory forevermore.

Read
Zephaniah 3:14–20.

Spirit, thank you for
the joy that can only be
found in you.

MAY 19

The LORD says, "Shout and rejoice, O beautiful Jerusalem, for I am coming to live among you."

—**Zechariah 2:10** (NLT)

A PRESENCE OF JOY

The Father promised he would come to Jerusalem, and that promise was fulfilled. I am here. When I dwell in you, the Father does too. The moment I came upon you, you were given a seat among the heavenly hosts. You accepted the promise of eternity and will now dwell with the Father forever. Praise the Most High! Take heart and delight in my presence.

Through me the Father dwells in you, and in his presence there is nothing to fear. Do not allow this world to pull you away from him, for it will not last. The pains of today will have no hold in eternity.

Take this victory into the world. The Son was crucified so all may know the Father. Every person deserves this delight. Share with those around you the joy of the Father, so they may celebrate with you in my presence.

Read
Zechariah 2:10–11.

Help me bring your joy to a world in need, so I may rejoice in victory with those around me.

MAY 20

The women ran quickly from the tomb. They were very frightened but also filled with great joy.

—**Matthew 28:8** (NLT)

THE JOY OF THE RESURRECTION

I saw the empty tomb, and I rejoiced with the women who came to behold the risen Son. The Resurrection was celebrated by multitudes. It brought joy to the disciples, and it will bring joy to all believers until the end of the age. I give that joy to any who ask for it.

I was with the Son during his time on earth, and he, in his joy, returned to heaven so that I could come and be with you. Now, I bring the joy of the resurrected Son into every person who reaches for my overflowing cup.

I manifest myself in your heart and teach you. I spread the love and healing paid for by the Son's sacrifice. Reach out and experience the joy I am offering you today.

Read Matthew 28:1–8.

Let me remember Christ through the joy that I can now have through the Spirit.

*Then the angel said to them,
"Do not be afraid, for behold,
I bring you good tidings of
great joy which will be to all
people."*

—**Luke 2:10** (NKJV)

THE JOY OF JESUS' BIRTH

When Jesus, the incarnate form of the Son, was
born, heaven erupted in joy. The angels brought
good news. With the birth of Jesus, the Father's plan was
heading toward its climax.

The Father commanded one of his angels to herald
the joyful news to some shepherds on the hills outside
of Bethlehem. The joy of that birth was meant to be
delivered "to all." The joy of Jesus' birth meant that
God's creation, the sons and daughters of Adam and Eve,
might be able to join the Father in heaven.

Dear one, embrace the joy that the Father has given
to you through the birth of Jesus. Share that joy with
someone today.

Read
Luke 2:8–20.

*Help me to embrace the joy
of Jesus' birth and to spread
that joy to others.*

As the Father has loved Me, I have also loved you. Remain in My love.

—**John 15:9** (HCSB)

REMAIN

The Son is the true Vine and the Father is the Vineyard Keeper. My presence and love keep you attached to the Vine—fully engrafted into the family of God.

Jesus commanded his disciples to remain in his love. I see the wheels turning in your head, wondering how you can keep such a command. Just as a weaker branch must be connected to the stronger vine in order to produce the most fruit, so I keep you connected to Jesus with the same goal. You are able to remain in his love because I remain in you.

Beloved, nothing will ever separate us. It is my great delight to produce bountiful fruit in your life to the glory of the Son.

Read John 15:1–17.

I'm grateful, God, for the work you do to keep me secure in the love of Christ.

The disciples were filled with
joy and with the Holy Spirit.
—**Acts 13:52** (ESV)

FILLED WITH JOY

Paul, Barnabas, and many others in biblical times faced trials amid the spreading of the Word and the planting of churches. Not everyone accepted the truth as fact. Yet Jesus' love defined their actions and gave them an identity to cling to, despite opposition. The power of the gospel and its message consumed Jesus' followers with joy. They learned to carry on in the face of rejection, knowing that the gospel was too important to be silenced by a mob.

I long to fill you with that same joy, a joy that drowns out the voices of dissension and misery. This joy transcends pain and sorrow and remains with you even through the darkest days of your life.

Be filled with and comforted by the gladness I provide today.

Read
Acts 13:44–52.

Father, fill me to the brim
with your joy.

*The kingdom of God is not
eating and drinking, but
righteousness and peace and
joy in the Holy Spirit.*

—**Romans 14:17** (NASB)

JOY IN ME

Singing and dancing, eating and drinking—these
activities make a person happy for the short-term.
But joy involves doing what is right and being at peace
with God. Child, you cannot gain joy from anything the
world produces. Only my work in you can produce joy
that lasts for eternity.

Joy is a flower that grows despite the soil of sorrow
in a life. I water it with my wisdom and fertilize it with my
love. Soon, joy spreads like ivy from your soul to that of
another. It is a gift that keeps on giving.

Beloved, as a citizen of the kingdom of God, I can
make you sing with gladness, despite the hurts in your
life. Don't settle for the short-term fixes the world offers.
Wait for the joy I will gladly give you.

**Read
Romans 14:13–23.**

*Heavenly Spirit, help
me to focus on your
righteousness, peace, and
joy today.*

[Love] does not rejoice at wrongdoing, but rejoices with the truth.

—**1 Corinthians 13:6** (ESV)

SEEK TRUTH

L ove has many characteristics, and one of them is that it finds great joy in the truth. While truth can seem to be quite elusive (remember that Pontius Pilate asked Jesus at the trial, "What is truth?" [John 18:38 ESV]), there are times when you simply know in your heart when something is wrong and when something is right. How does that happen? It's me, guiding you and showing you.

Many will search for the path to truth, but not all will find it. The world will try to tell you differently. But there is only one path to truth—through Christ, the Savior, who called himself "the way, and the truth, and the life" (John 14:6 ESV).

Child of God, the Father rejoices because you have found truth! The moment you trusted in God, I took up residence within you. I am here, beloved, helping you know the truth. What glory and delight you bring to your Father by walking in the truth!

**Read
1 Corinthians 13.**

Lord, please help me know and stand firm in the truth today.

We want to work together with
you so you will be full of joy.

—2 Corinthians 1:24 (NLT)

FULL OF JOY

I love to see my people working together joyfully. I am thrilled when the people in a church, a ministry, or any small group of believers serve together, each person using the spiritual gifts I gave to him or her. I am pleased to fit the gifts together, like a puzzle, and I enjoy creating such groups, assembling the people needed to accomplish a task for God's kingdom.

Too often, however, believers spend time arguing over "power" positions or particular details that are so much less important than reaching out to a needy world with the message of eternal salvation. The apostle Paul was sensitive to the Christians in Corinth, yet he also understood the importance of not letting arguments get in the way of sharing the good news.

As you work with others, focus on the gifts I give and help people serve out of their gifts. Then all of you will be able to work together and be full of joy!

Read
2 Corinthians
1:18–2:4.

Lord, may the Spirit
bring me joy through
working with and
serving others.

MAY 27

*I thank my God upon every
remembrance of you, always
in every prayer of mine
for you all making request
with joy.*

—Philippians 1:3–4 (KJV)

JOYFUL PRAYER

When Paul wrote to churches to tell them his vision for spreading the gospel, he exhorted them with love and hope. He spoke of his trials, but in praying through me, he found joy in praying for others.

In the opening prayer of Philippians, Paul's words overflow with this joy. He prays in love, and he thanks God for the joy it gives him.

Paul points believers in the right direction. Often, Christians pray for comfort and assistance in their own lives. This is necessary and good, but think of the joy Paul found in praying for others. It was a way of looking with Christ's eyes at the people he loved dearly.

Whom will you joyfully pray for today?

**Read
Philippians 1:3–11.**

*Lord, help me to find joy in
praying for others.*

MAY 28

[Be] strengthened with all power according to his glorious might so that you may have great endurance and patience, ... giving joyful thanks to the Father.
—**Colossians 1:11–12** (NIV)

COME TO ME

The ways of the world are trying, dear one. Stay close to me and live your life worthy of my love. Everything you do, do it for righteousness and you will grow in your knowledge and understanding of the kingdom. If you do good works for my sake, I will strengthen you when you are weary and help you to carry on.

Through my glorious power, you will endure. I will not give you more than you have the strength to handle. When you overcome adversity and trials, give thanks. I have provided for you in abundance—my love and my inheritance. When your earthly body passes away, you will join all the saints in the heavenly kingdom, a place that would blind your earthly eyes.

I have rescued you from what is evil and sinful. Follow me, and you will come from the darkness into the light.

Read Colossians 1:9–14.

Show me how to follow you, divine Spirit. Teach me your ways and give me your strength to follow them.

MAY 29

Your love has given me much joy and comfort, my brother, for your kindness has often refreshed the hearts of God's people.

—Philemon 7 (NLT)

FRIENDSHIP BRINGS JOY

God designed people for relationships. Your desire for companionship in friendship, marriage, and work comes from the One who created you. That's one reason he gave Adam a partner in Eve—because he knew it was not good for Adam to be alone (Genesis 2:18).

Paul understood the importance of friendship, thanking God every day for his friendships with his brothers and sisters in Christ. He was thankful for those who cared for him and who also went about loving others.

God has placed friends and loved ones around you for a reason. You are meant to bring comfort and joy to one another in a way that material things cannot. A friend knows you and wants what is best for you. Remember: you can rely on your fellow believers when I bring you together.

Read Philemon 1–7.

Thank you for the friends you have placed in my life. Help me to be a good friend to others.

MAY 30

That which was from the beginning, which we have heard, which we have seen with our eyes . . .

—1 John 1:1 (NKJV)

SHARING TRUTH

Beloved, don't believe the false reports of those who claim to know God yet know nothing of Jesus.

As John proclaimed, he had walked with Jesus during the Son's years on earth—sharing in his joys and heartaches, watching his miraculous deeds with awe, listening to the profundity of his teachings. He believed that the Son was the promised Messiah, having been with Jesus from the beginning of his ministry to the end of his days on earth.

In the same way, you can be a witness to the truth by your life. Only you can share how Jesus has changed your life. I can help you remember your experiences—the joys and sorrows—as you follow Jesus.

Read
1 John 1:1–4.

Lord, help me make my experiences of you tangible to others.

MAY 31

Now to Him who is able to keep you from stumbling, and to make you stand in the presence of His glory blameless with great joy . . .

—Jude 24 (NASB)

JOY IN THE JOURNEY

Even when surrounded by doubters, mockers, and scoffers, the children of God have hope.

Child, take my hand. You do not have to retreat. Stay close to me today. Let me guard you. Keep yourself in my love. My footing is sure. I do not stumble.

And then follow my gaze. Do you see it? Heaven. Glorious heaven! It's waiting. In heaven, sin falls away. Spotless. Faultless. Blameless. What a joyous celebration that will be.

Rejoice in it now! And let that joy—my joy—guide your steps as we go into battle today. I know you can. Already I see a smile beginning to dance around your mouth and your eyes starting to sparkle. I see your spirits lifting as we get ready to go on the offensive together against doubters, mockers, and scoffers.

Come, take my hand. The war isn't over, but there is joy in the journey because we know what glory awaits!

Read
Jude 17–25.

Holy Spirit, let your joy fill my steps today as I look to the glory of heaven.

JUNE

The Fruit of the Spirit: Peace

JUNE 1

*The Holy Spirit produces this
kind of fruit in our lives:...
peace.*

—**Galatians 5:22** (NLT)

SAVOR THE FRUIT CALLED PEACE

Noise drives away peace. That's why people often head to the quiet spots and open places for rest. Without finding a moment alone, a bit of sweet silence, how can you hope to hear the Savior's call?

I offer you the fruit called peace. My gift goes far beyond stillness, however. It penetrates to a place that passes human knowledge. Tasting my peace means having a soul-deep understanding that Jesus loves you. It means knowing that he died for you and that you will live out eternity in his presence.

True peace means realizing finally that you are loved for all time. That you are forgiven. What solitude of the soul you will find as you taste the fruit of peace! I offer it to you, child. Turn from the noise, open your heart, and accept my gift.

**Read
Galatians 5:16–26.**

*Peace is not just a symbol
or a word. Give me lasting
peace in my heart, Lord.*

JUNE 2

Peace I leave with you. My peace
I give to you. I do not give to you
as the world gives. Your heart
must not be troubled or fearful.

—**John 14:27** (HCSB)

THE SPIRIT'S PEACE

I do not settle for half measures. When the Son promised the peace of God to those who followed him, he didn't mean the world's definition of peace. My peace is more than just the absence of worry or strife. It is a tangible calm, a reality to be grasped and wielded for God's kingdom. That's because my peace is a person. Like the Son, I give of myself to you.

The world pretends that you can have an easy life of comfort. You can't—there will be struggles always. But I stand beside you as the God of all peace. In me, there is no fear or worry.

The world can comfort you physically, but it also torments your mind and soul at times. I can give your mind and soul peace in me.

Read
John 14:23–31.

God, thank you for giving me peace. I'm grateful that no power in heaven or earth can possibly take away your peace.

Therefore, having been justified by faith, we have peace with God through our Lord Jesus Christ.

—Romans 5:1 (NASB)

A HOLY TURNCOAT

Do you remember the days when you were my enemy? I loved you and sought you day after day, even when you had set your face against me. It broke my heart to see your unwillingness to accept what could fulfill you.

Child, you have no idea the joy I felt when you turned to me. As soon as you looked to me, I rushed to embrace you. Your faith in Christ was all it took, and you became mine. I came to dwell in you and claimed you as my own for eternity.

Jesus' sacrifice presented you as a holy, pleasing offering. You can't understand how I longed to call you my own and how incredible it was to at last welcome you into our family.

Dear one, someday, when you enter our presence in heaven, I promise you will hear the angelic chorus rejoicing like they did the moment you were justified before the Father.

**Read
Romans 5:1–11.**

Lord, thank you for accepting and loving me.

JUNE 4

To set the mind on the flesh is death, but to set the mind on the Spirit is life and peace.

—**Romans 8:6** (ESV)

PEACE OF MIND

I am the Spirit of wisdom and the Spirit of truth. I am your Comforter and Counselor. You cannot see my desires and plan for your life, but I have your greatest fulfillment in mind. Trust me when I say that your mind is a sacred place. If you focus on my will and voice, you will have life and peace through me.

Why do you hold on to burdens and distractions? Why do you carry all that weight? Lay it down. A burdensome life is not what I have in mind for you. I offer you vitality, but instead you choose things that lead to death.

Lay all your burdens in this world at the cross of Jesus. Give me your worries and fears, and then rise to live for God and leave all that dead weight behind.

Read Romans 8:5–9.

Give me peace of mind today. Help me to leave my "dead" weight of worry and fears behind as I look to you, Lord.

JUNE 5

For the kingdom of God is not a matter of eating and drinking but of righteousness and peace and joy in the Holy Spirit.

—**Romans 14:17** (ESV)

PEACE THROUGH THE SPIRIT

I was distressed to see the disorderly conduct of the early church. Many members were overcome with anxiety as they questioned whether they could eat meat sacrificed to idols. This controversy turned to judgment, and judgment turned to quarreling. The enemy used this small seed of doubt to disrupt the unity of the body and to discourage many of its members. But Paul's peaceful example restored relationships among the brethren.

Loved one, we desire peace, unity, and order among all our children—including you. Approach every situation with a gentle attitude. Settle matters of conscience peacefully, and do not quarrel with your brothers and sisters in Christ.

Look to me for peace in your heart and harmony in your interactions. It brings me joy when you serve me this way.

Read
Romans 14:13–18.

Lord, I desire the peace that you provide. Help me live in peaceful harmony with others today and every day.

JUNE 6

For he himself is our peace, who has made the two groups one and has destroyed the barrier, the dividing wall of hostility.

—**Ephesians 2:14** (NIV)

NO BARRIERS BETWEEN US

I see the walls that divide individual from individual: the fences; the defenses of the heart; the chains of mistrust; the prejudice and hatred. They deeply grieve me, child. I long for everyone to know of the solution: Jesus. He made peace possible between God and people, between people and other people.

In Christ, there are no barriers. All are one—unified by the blood he shed on the cross. This destroying of dividing walls and healing of hostilities brings me great joy.

Allow me, dear one, to take a hammer to the walls that separate you from the Father and from others. And then, by faith, you will experience my peace and see all Christians as I see them: one people unified by the Son.

Read
Ephesians 2:11–22.

Lord, in your mercy, tear down the walls of my heart that divide me from others, and give me peace.

JUNE 7

When the Messiah came, He proclaimed the good news of peace to you who were far away and peace to those who were near.

—**Ephesians 2:17** (HCSB)

THE PEACE GOD OFFERS

In a world bent toward evil and chaos, you sometimes find yourself wondering where I am in the midst of the confusion. If I were truly there, you rationalize, I wouldn't allow certain things to happen. Child, I bring peace, but not always according to your definition of peace. Since you live in a fallen world, it is impossible for you to find peace by turning to worldly vanities. But do not worry. I promise you a righteous peace—a spiritual satisfaction that transcends the noise, anger, and confusion of your world. Commune with me and allow the calmness of a caring God to minister to you when you are agitated, confused, or overwhelmed. Exchange the chaos for spiritual serenity. I offer it to you daily. Call upon me.

Remember, I am with you always, and I have been teaching believers the good news of peace for thousands of years.

Read Ephesians 2:17–18.

Holy Spirit, take my worries and fears and lay them to rest. I trust you to carry me and to give me peace.

JUNE 8

Make every effort to keep yourselves united in the Spirit, binding yourselves together with peace.

—**Ephesians 4:3** (NLT)

DESIRE PEACE

Are you eager for peace? Are you eager to hear my call to be like Christ and to consider others as greater than yourself? I am the bond that holds the church together. I am with all of your brothers and sisters in Christ, just as I am with you.

When you argue with one another, I grieve. Disunity is the consequence of misunderstanding and a focus on differences. Child, you don't have to subscribe to the world's views when dealing with those around you. Instead, if you focus on Christ, the differences will fall away and you will be able to maintain peace.

Trust in the peace that belongs to all who are humble in me. This peace cannot be ignored, and it binds the saints to face any trial.

What can you do today to "make every effort" to bring peace to a stressful situation?

Read Ephesians 4:2–7.

Lord, please inspire a desire in me for humility and peace.

The peace of God, which surpasses all understanding, will guard your hearts and minds through Christ Jesus.

—**Philippians 4:7** (NKJV)

PEACE: GUARDIAN OF THE HEART

D o not let your heart be anxious. My peace, the peace of the Father, is with you. Because the Son sacrificed himself for you, there is no trouble that the joy of the Father cannot overcome.

I will defend you against all troubles and burdens if you will but ask, believing and trusting in the Father's will for you. Rejoice, for the Father embraces you with his love.

Your life will not always be joyful. In this world trials will come, but take heart. When you are overwhelmed by the burdens of this life, call upon the Lord in thanksgiving, faith, and humility. The Son will hear your cry and relay your words to the Father, and I will provide peace for you. Your heart will no longer be burdened and sorrowful. It will rest in the Father's love and be full of his joy. Let my peace be the guardian of your heart.

Read
Philippians 4:4–7.

Guard my heart with your peace, so I may face today with your joy.

JUNE 10

Show them great respect and
wholehearted love because of
their work. And live peacefully
with each other.

—**1 Thessalonians 5:13** (NLT)

VALUE WHAT YOU PROCLAIM

Many of you struggle within the body of Christ, squabbling over worship styles, who is in charge of what, how things should be run, and so on. Over time these disputes about unimportant things begin to distance you from one another. It grieves me to see this happen.

I challenge you to make every effort to put aside your differences with others and work together in the church, respecting one another for the ways in which you each serve. No two people will ever agree on every point. It is pointless to try to make it so. Worse, it is fruitless because you could be drawing on your differences to serve more fully instead of wasting time in debate.

Make every attempt to maintain peace among yourselves so others will see that you value what you proclaim. This will bring glory to God.

Read
1 Thessalonians
5:12–22.

Lord, help me to love,
show respect toward, and
work in peace with those
who serve you.

JUNE 11

Now flee from youthful lusts and pursue righteousness, faith, love and peace, with those who call on the Lord from a pure heart.

—**2 Timothy 2:22** (NASB)

PURSUE PEACE

You are a spiritual being. This is the way you were created. It is through your spirit that I talk to you and guide you. You sense in your spirit when I am nudging you to take action or when I want you to fix what is wrong. When your spirit is not at peace, I am speaking to you, telling you that there is something you must do or realize.

Sometimes you ignore me because you don't want to know what I have to say, or because you simply don't want to listen. I wish you wouldn't ignore me. Here is my promise: I will never ask you to do something that is not for your ultimate benefit.

If I want you to remove something from your life, it is not to deprive you of this thing, but rather to provide you with what is better in its absence! Trust that I love you. Then trust that you will have peace when you pursue the better things.

**Read
2 Timothy 2:20–26.**

Holy Spirit, help me to flee from things that are wrong and to live in your peace and righteousness today.

JUNE 12

I will give peace to the land, and you will lie down with nothing to frighten you. I will remove dangerous animals from the land, and no sword will pass through your land.

—**Leviticus 26:6** (HCSB)

THE PATH OF PEACE

Our people, the Israelites, faced a long journey from Egypt to the Promised Land, from slavery to freedom. They were unsure of what lay ahead. As they stood on the threshold of becoming a nation, they had a choice—to follow a path of obedience or disobedience. The way was clearly set before them. If they would obey our commands, we would shower them with blessings and bring peace to their land. If they disobeyed, they would face certain punishment—drought, disease, attacks from their enemies.

The same path is set before you. As you seek to follow God's commands, I will bring you peace. You will not need to fear anyone or anything. You need not toss and turn at night—nothing will frighten you. I dwell within your heart and am with you every moment. I give you everlasting life and will keep you secure.

Which path will you choose today?

Read Leviticus 26:1–13.

Spirit, help me choose the path of obedience today. Fill me with your peace as I live in obedience to your commands.

JUNE 13

The LORD bless you and keep you; the LORD make his face shine on you and be gracious to you; the LORD turn his face toward you and give you peace.

—**Numbers 6:24–26** (NIV)

MY BLESSING

"God bless you." You have spoken these words many times and have heard them from your pastor, a friend, or a parent as you embarked upon a new venture. A blessing, whether you are offering it or receiving it, is a way to encourage someone, to show them love and compassion. And so it was that I gave words of blessing to Moses and Aaron as a way to remind them and God's chosen children of our special care and love for them.

Ask for my blessing today, and I will freely give you my hand of protection. I will smile upon you and shower you with grace, and I will show you my favor as a child of God, granting you my peace.

Beloved, you belong to God. Be blessed with favor and peace.

**Read
Numbers 6:22–27.**

Thank you, God, for your blessing of protection, favor, grace, and your peace.

JUNE 14

*The LORD has held you back
from coming to bloodshed and
from avenging yourself with
your own hand.*

—1 Samuel 25:26 (NKJV)

ACTIONS THAT RESULT IN PEACE

As the Spirit of godly love, I give abundant blessings to those who create peace. Abigail humbled herself before David in order to hold him back from revenge against her cruel husband. As I did with Abigail, I reward peacemakers with protection, forgiveness, blessings, and honor.

Peace isn't always the natural state of things in your world, and sometimes you need to act in decisive ways in order to help bring peace. Perhaps it's offering a gracious gesture when that's the last thing you feel like doing, saying an encouraging word when angry words come to mind, or simply responding to an insult with kindness. These are the types of actions that can bring peace to a potentially explosive situation.

I am honored when you seek peace as much as possible. You cannot control the responses of others, but *you*, at least, can be my agent of peace. Seek peace, and let me do the rest.

Read
1 Samuel 25:23–35.

*Lord, let your Spirit of
grace fall upon me as I
show kindness to others.*

JUNE 15

*Submit to God and be at
peace with him; in this way
prosperity will come to you.*

—**Job 22:21** (NIV)

PEACE IN SUBMISSION

I know the troubles of the world. I was there when sin
first entered. I have watched the enemy oppress the
people of God. I have watched sin suppress the joy of
those who follow Christ. I tell you that even righteous
people such as Job have been oppressed by sin and
the troubles of the world. Job lost everything he had—
everything but his soul.

Despite all his worldly afflictions, Job found peace
in accepting God's sovereignty. In doing so, he received
more than he lost; he even lived to see his great-great-
grandchildren. You too can be at peace with the Father if
you submit to the will of God.

Like Job, the troubles of this world will oppress you,
but never fear. Submit to God and be at peace with him.

**Read
Job 22:15–27.**

*Lord, I crave the peace you
offer. Help me submit my
will to you.*

JUNE 16

The LORD will give strength unto his people; the LORD will bless his people with peace.

—**Psalm 29:11** (KJV)

RELY ON ME

Dearest child, I allow you to go through trials, but not because I want to see you in pain or don't love you. On the contrary, I allow you to experience difficulties *because* I love you and want you to draw closer to me.

I gave my servant David the strength to keep going despite the many attempts Saul made on his life. David knew firsthand the strength and peace I provide in the toughest of times.

I know the thought of hardship can be frightening. You don't have to allow fear to gain mastery over you, however. I will be with you every moment, leading you, holding your hand.

Though your struggles can seem overwhelming, don't be afraid to call on me. I will give you the strength and peace you need to face any challenge.

Read Psalm 29.

Spirit of love, as I face trials, help me rely on you to be my strength and peace.

JUNE 17

Depart from evil and do good;
seek peace and pursue it.

—**Psalm 34:14** (NKJV)

CHOOSE PEACE

Beloved, every day you pass signs telling you the way to go or the proper way to behave: Walk. Don't Walk. Yield. Do Not Enter. Ignoring those signs can cause chaos. Yet the choice to obey them is still yours. No one else can make that choice for you.

Likewise, each day you face a choice: to do good or to do evil. Peace or chaos comes as a result of whatever choice you make. I long for you to make the choice to do good and to seek peace.

Beloved, as you choose to follow me rather than the evil one, know that you are honoring your Father. And today, as you find peace, know that I am at work.

Read Psalm 34.

Father, today I choose to follow you. Help me seek holiness and goodness through my thoughts and actions.

Mark the blameless man, and
observe the upright; for the
future of that man is peace.

—**Psalm 37:37** (NKJV)

A NEW PERSPECTIVE

Many people strive to have a good reputation, to be seen by others as "good" and upright. They pride themselves on appearances. Yet, child, to be truly upright, you need a Savior.

I can show you those who are truly blameless before me. The blameless are those whose faces radiate the peace that I provide. The blameless are not perfect. Instead, they are truly aware of their fallen nature. Yet they know the one who is truly without fault: Jesus. Instead of living life according to their sinful flesh, those who are upright live according to my guidance.

A sinful outlook leads to death, but I bring life and peace as you look to me for a new perspective. Dear one, know that this perspective pleases the Father.

Today, no matter what you are going through, you can be refreshed, for I have breathed new life into you. And with it you will know everlasting peace.

Read
Psalm 37.

Lord, you took the blame
for my sin, so that I can
be blameless before you.

JUNE 19

Deceit is in the heart of those who devise evil, but counselors of peace have joy.

—**Proverbs 12:20** (NKJV)

PEACE PREVAILS

Child, I have heard you ask why those who do evil are not held accountable, why they sometimes even prosper. Presidents of corporations close businesses and revoke pensions, yet they manage to retain their expensive lifestyles. Criminals steal identities and life savings, yet they don't get caught. Kids bully other kids but aren't held accountable for their behavior.

Be assured those deeds are not going unnoticed. If the Father is aware of each sparrow that falls from the sky (Matthew 10:29), how much more is he aware of the suffering of his most precious creation? Therefore, don't repay evil for evil (Romans 12:17). Don't plan to get back at someone who hurts you. Do what is right in the sight of the Lord and the law, and be at peace, knowing that our justice will eventually prevail—not in your timing, but in heaven's.

Leave it all in my hands. Be at peace, and experience the resulting joy.

Read Proverbs 12:20–28.

Lord, I know you are in control. Help me to be at peace as you work out your justice.

JUNE 20

Correct your son, and he will give you rest; yes, he will give delight to your soul.

—**Proverbs 29:17** (NKJV)

DISCIPLINE BRINGS PEACE

*D*iscipline means to train, to develop, to correct. A child needs to be trained not to touch a hot stovetop or run into the road. If he is not trained, the consequences will be disastrous. A child needs to be disciplined to be obedient and faithful. Good parents train, correct, and discipline their children because they love them!

Likewise, I train and correct you because you are beloved of God. When you accept my discipline, you bring peace to the kingdom. When you apply what I am teaching you, you bring peace to yourself and delight to your soul.

Through your obedience and faithfulness to God, you enjoy the fruit of peace.

Read Proverbs 29:1, 3, 17, 21.

Lord, give me wisdom as I discipline the children in my care and respond to your discipline of me.

JUNE 21

A time to love and a time to hate, a time for war and a time for peace.

—**Ecclesiastes 3:8** (NIV)

TIMING AND TAPESTRY

I was there when the Father set time in motion. I was there when He decided to let freedom and divine will coexist. There is a time for everything. Oh, the rich pattern and design that each choice, situation, and event brings to the tapestry of life! And I love when you include me in your choices as the pattern of your life is woven.

Talk to me today about your choices. You will have them, you know. Start here, in this moment. I'm listening. A warrior? A peacemaker? Which will you be today?

Your day comes from God. But you are not unprepared. I will guide you. I will give you direction. All you have to do is ask. Turn to me today as you face each situation. My wisdom and discernment are waiting. And there is a time for everything—including peace.

Read
Ecclesiastes 3:1–8.

Holy Spirit, give me discernment and discretion for the right thing in the right time.

JUNE 22

*His name will be called
Wonderful Counselor, Mighty
God, Eternal Father, Prince of
Peace.*

—Isaiah 9:6 (NASB)

A PROMISE OF PEACE

Turmoil. Chaos. Disorder. After years of apostasy,
Israel was a scattered nation. Because they were
spiritually far from me, God's people lost their homeland,
one of the things most important to them.

I guided the prophets who encouraged the people to
repent. Through Isaiah, I gave the promise of the Savior,
whose very essence would be peace.

In the midst of the world's turmoil, the Father sent
his Son to offer peace. As you submit to him, he will bring
peace to you as well.

You can have peace because Christ has come and is
coming again. Someday he will rule forever as the Prince
of Peace.

Read
Isaiah 9:1–7.

*Lord, help me find time
to dwell on your peace
and thank you for your
rest.*

Behold, on the mountains the feet of him who brings good news, who announces peace!

—**Nahum 1:15** (NASB)

GOOD NEWS!

The news headlines usually do not announce good news. The world in which you live is fraught with heartache, turmoil, and war. Precious one, don't despair. I have been to the mountain and looked beyond the summit. What I see is cause for much celebration and joy.

I have good news to bring. You have reason to rejoice. The Father is in control. Those in conflict will lay down their weapons. It's just a matter of time.

You see, beloved, I am the heartbeat of the Creator— and with every beat of his heart, the rhythm of peace pulsates in the world. I am the Spirit of peace, and if you will quiet your heart every day, emptying yourself of your anxiety and anger, you will be a conduit of my peace, bringing the good news to others as you go about your daily tasks.

Read
Nahum 1:12–15.

Lord, fill me with peace that I will be a peaceful presence wherever I go today.

JUNE 24

The future glory of this Temple will be greater than its past glory, says the LORD of Heaven's Armies. And in this place I will bring peace.

—**Haggai 2:9** (NLT)

HEAVENLY PEACE!

I filled Solomon's temple after that magnificent structure took shape. From breathtaking blueprints the Father imagined to the glimmering gold edifice that emerged, I cheered my delight. It was a house of prayer. It was also a house of peace. It was a house of worship unlike any other.

But that temple was destroyed. So was the replica King Herod built in its place. The conflict that flowed out of selfish hearts and warring nations destroyed this magnificent symbol of divine presence. But the original blueprints have not been misplaced. My peace will return as a future temple is completed. The glory of the old will be dwarfed by the wonder of the new.

Trust me, dear one. Trust my peace and rest in it.

Read
Haggai 2:4–9.

Spirit of peace, make my heart a temple of your presence this day.

*Salt is good; but if the salt
becomes unsalty, with what
will you make it salty again?
Have salt in yourselves, and
be at peace with one another.*
—**Mark 9:50** (NASB)

INTRICATELY DESIGNED

Dear one, you were made special. You are more
intricately designed than a snowflake, yet every part
of you is just as unique. You were created to have precious
qualities that make you a blessing to those around you.
Do not compare yourself to others. You were meant to be
exactly the way you are.

The trials and temptations you undergo make you
distinctive. They make you "salty," with a unique and
pleasant seasoning that flavors your life. This is something
I give to you as well. This seasoning allows you to have
your own perspective on following me and to have wisdom
others might lack.

Take what you have learned from your past and
apply it. Because you are loved, you can be at peace with
one another.

Read
Mark 9:47–50.

*Guiding Spirit, allow
me to see the good in my
differences, and help me to
stay true to my salty design.*

To give light to those who sit in darkness and in the shadow of death, to guide our feet into the way of peace.

—Luke 1:79 (ESV)

GOD GUIDES IN PEACE

Beloved, consider the joy you feel when you're lost in the darkness and stumble across a light. From the beginning the plan was for the life of John the Baptist to be a guiding light to those who were lost in darkness. His father, Zechariah, sang of the ministry his son would have. John the Baptist preached a message of repentance to prepare the hearts of people to receive the coming Savior, the Prince of Peace. The Father knew the people's pain and affliction, and he was ready to help them.

Through the shadows and the doubts, through the bad days and trials, I will guide your feet into the way of peace. You may not know where you are going, but I am dwelling inside you. I will take you where I want you to go.

Read Luke 1:78–79.

Lord, shower me with peace and guide my feet down your chosen path.

JUNE 27

Here on earth you will have many trials and sorrows. But take heart, because I have overcome the world.

—**John 16:33** (NLT)

ALWAYS WITH YOU

Jesus' words resonate with you. Many trials and sorrows? I know you know all about that, for I've seen your tears, your frustration, your turmoil. Trials and sorrows are just part of life in a fallen world. But just as Jesus spoke words of triumph to his followers in his day, he spoke them to you. He didn't leave his beloved in turmoil, without guidance. He wanted you to know that the current state of the world is not forever. He has overcome!

After he returned to heaven, the Son sent me—his Holy Spirit—to be with those who love him. Forever. Down through the ages for all who accept me, I have whispered peace into the souls of those crying for it—including yours. I fulfill the promise of a Comforter (John 14:26 KJV). I gently guide you into realizing that no matter what cyclone is spinning around you, Jesus is in control.

Allow my peace to flood every aspect of your life as you acknowledge Jesus as Lord.

Read John 16:29–33.

Holy Spirit, fall on me. Wash away my worry with your promised peace.

JUNE 28

So then, dear friends, since you are looking forward to this, make every effort to be found spotless, blameless and at peace with him.

—2 Peter 3:14 (NIV)

TRUST ME FOR PEACE

I watch you. I discern your thoughts. Precious one, even though you may not voice your despair—your frustrated and sometimes accusing questions—I read them on your heart: *God, why? Why do you allow this to happen? To me? To my loved ones?*

Full understanding of life's trials will not be unveiled until the time is right—perhaps not even in your lifetime. But as a child of God with your eyes on the promise of a new heaven and a new earth, allow me into the depths of your soul to keep peace with your Creator.

Jesus reconciled you to God by his death and resurrection. I seal your relationship with God by my stamp of faith and belief. Yielding to my presence increases your trust and bestows blessed peace with God and all the marvelous things he's working for good in your life.

**Read
2 Peter 3:8–18.**

Forgive me for questioning your lordship! Holy Spirit, I accept and thank you for the gift of peace.

JUNE 29

For the moment all discipline seems painful rather than pleasant, but later it yields the peaceful fruit of righteousness to those who have been trained by it.

—**Hebrews 12:11** (ESV)

PEACE FROM ENDURANCE

Any training period of your life includes aspects that are unpleasant—the swift sting of a parent's swat to steer you away from danger, dreaded tests in school, mistakes made at a new job. But every single time that you hang in there and stay on course, you become stronger, wiser, and more mature. Another small blinder comes off your inexperienced eyes and another step is added to your race to the finish line—the complete person God is designing you to be.

Sink deep into that realization. Nothing has changed. Consider whatever trials you are facing right now to be a training ground where you invest blood, sweat, and tears. Giving your all will lead to fruit in your life when you open the blessed exit door of the arena, equipped with the strength and peace to make a difference in your world.

Read Hebrews 12:3–13.

I want your power, Holy Spirit, to continue my training and to enjoy peace in the process.

JUNE 30

*And the fruit of righteousness
is sown in peace by those who
cultivate peace.*

—James 3:18 (HCSB)

CONTAGIOUS PEACE

You've seen it before. A light and cheery mood soured
by someone else's acidic remark. An anxious person
encouraged by sharing gut-busting laughter with a
sensitive friend. A spirit of apathy changed into passion
because a flame of motivation burned among family
members.

People affect people. Think of what my peace
working through you can do.

When you yield to my wonder-working power and
allow my security to embolden you, others around you
see it. You can effect change in their lives in a myriad
of situations. If you are the calm in the chaos at work,
coworkers will notice. If you are the faithful supplier of
water on the soccer field, thirsty bodies will seek you. If
you are the pioneer of new ideas, others will follow. The
peace you emanate will spread to them, cultivating the
peace of the Spirit in a world desperately needing it.

Read
James 3:13–18.

*Holy Spirit, fill me with
your peace to overflowing
so that it spills into the
lives around me.*

JULY

THE FRUIT OF THE SPIRIT: PATIENCE

JULY 1

*The fruit of the Spirit is . . .
patience.*

—**Galatians 5:22** (NASB)

SAVOR THE FRUIT CALLED PATIENCE

People plead for patience but are unwilling to wait.
Let me tell you a secret: this flavorful fruit is one few
want. I understand why, for the investment is steep. How
wonderful it would be to sit down and play a concerto
without any practice, or to sow a seed and see a tree
heavy with fruit the next morning. Such is the stuff of
fairy tales.

Only years of practice produce perfect music. The
mustard-sized seed must gradually mature before it
can flower. Rushing patience isn't possible! In an era of
texting, instant headlines, and fast-food meals, I can see
why many balk at the time required to develop patience.
Sadly, patience is out of style, even among believers.

Stand against the masses, child. Learn to wait.
Understand that it may be better to start something
worthwhile than to finish a million unimportant endeavors.

Read
**Galatians 5:16–26;
James 5:8.**

*Lord, please give me
opportunities to develop
the fruit of patience in
my life.*

JULY 2

*If anyone cleanses himself
from these things, he will be
a vessel for honor, sanctified,
useful to the Master, prepared
for every good work.*

—**2 Timothy 2:21** (NASB)

LIFE-GIVING PATIENCE

You are a beautiful vessel—just perfect for the work you were designed to do. Have you forgotten? I haven't. I've been interceding for you. The Father is patient and merciful. Now is the time to look to me, dust yourself off, and turn back to the way of righteousness you've been taught.

I want life for you, not destruction. I know you sometimes feel that the design of your vessel isn't right, useful, or wonderful. But trust me, it is.

I will gladly cleanse you today, starting from the inside out. You can work with me by confessing your need to be cleansed. Afterward, you can show others the fruit of patience that I have shown you. Guide others along the way from destruction to life.

**Read
2 Timothy 2:14–26.**

*Lord, thank you for your
patience. Help me to return
to your way today.*

JULY 3

*Be joyful in hope, patient in
affliction, faithful in prayer.*

—**Romans 12:12** (NIV)

BASIC INSTRUCTIONS

B eloved child, your emotions are meant to be your
servant, not your master. I know how difficult it can
be to experience the joy of your salvation when times are
difficult. But power and authority are yours through me.

I am the Comforter sent to you from the moment of
your salvation. Even before you were born, the heavens
echoed with songs of my love for you. In days of war and
days of peace, I am ready to pour out my joy upon you.
Use the joy I give you to remain faithful.

When affliction comes upon you, be patient. Model
yourself after the Son, who bore every burden. He did
this for more than just salvation! He suffered so that in all
things you might dwell in communion with God. Honor
him with your joy, your patience, and your prayers.

**Read
Romans 12:9–21.**

*Lord, help me to live the
life you've set before me.
Strengthen me to do your
will.*

JULY 4

*May you be strengthened
with all power, according
to his glorious might, for all
endurance and patience
with joy.*

—**Colossians 1:11** (ESV)

STRENGTHENED TO ENDURE

Beloved, if only you knew the depths of my love for
you! The enemy fills the air with lies about me. If
your obedience was all I wanted, why would the Son have
sacrificed himself?

Though you abide by my laws and produce good fruit,
I do not expect you to do so alone. I am refining you,
filling you with my power and authority. I know the weight
of the world and the heavy burden of sin. But I empower
you with the perseverance to bear what is necessary. I love
you, dear child, and I will not ask more of you than you
can bear. Trust in my faithfulness and love.

There will be things in this life you can't understand
yet. My thoughts are not your thoughts. Instead, dwell on
my love for you and experience the joyous peace of the
Lord.

Read
Colossians 1:9–20.

*God, let me experience your
power and glory in my life.
Let me be a holy servant of
your will.*

JULY 5

Be patient with everyone.

—1 Thessalonians 5:14 (NLT)

BE PATIENT

Child, I know the hustle and bustle of everyday life. Many people rush about, anxious and impatient with others. They yell and honk their horns, thinking they have power to speed up time or control life itself. They live their lives like pots boiling over. In their panic and worry, they lose sight of something very important: there is joy in the wait.

I provide the patience that causes you to work day after day with a child learning a new skill; to listen over and over to the same stories from someone older and lonely; to walk step by step alongside a friend in need. Let my patience fill you and give you the sweet taste of life that few choose to slow down long enough to drink.

Come, child. Sip my patience slowly and enjoy every moment of it.

Read
1 Thessalonians
5:12–24.

I need your patience and wisdom today, Lord.

JULY 6

Yet for this reason I found mercy, so that in me as the foremost, Jesus Christ might demonstrate His perfect patience as an example for those who would believe in Him for eternal life.

—1 Timothy 1:16 (NASB)

UNLIMITED PATIENCE

For years I watched Saul's treachery. I saw every act of violence he committed against God's people. I heard every insult he spouted against my name. This saddened me, but I knew the perfect time to call Saul into my service and transform him into the apostle Paul. I knew he would repent and serve me.

I have known you since the beginning of time, beloved. I've seen every misdeed you've ever committed and heard every ugly word you've ever uttered. Even now, after being given salvation, I watch you struggle with sin. These actions hurt, but when you ask for my forgiveness, I will grant it to you without delay. Just as I suffered long for Paul, so also will I suffer long for you.

Just as my love for you knows no bounds, my patience with you will never end.

Read 1 Timothy 1:12–17.

Lord, thank you for showing me unlimited patience.

JULY 7

The Lord ... is patient with you, not wanting anyone to perish, but everyone to come to repentance.

—**2 Peter 3:9** (NIV)

SHARE YOUR GOOD NEWS

One day the Son will come for you. On that day he will come suddenly, like a thief, and bring you home. However, until that day, you can look ahead in expectation. Part of this is making sure others are ready too.

I do not wish that any should be left on that day. My desire is for everyone on earth to be with the Son for eternity. That is where you come in. Your job, until the moment the Son returns, is to tell others of his life, death, resurrection, and certain coming. While you can't reach every person, you can reach those near you.

Just as you want to tell everyone when something good happens to you, tell them of the Son. Tell them of his love and what he did for you. That's good news only you can share.

Read 2 Peter 3:8–13.

Gracious Spirit, as the day draws near for Jesus' return, help me to lead others to the Son.

JULY 8

Regard the patience of our Lord as an opportunity for salvation.

—**2 Peter 3:15** (HCSB)

ACTIVE PATIENCE

After the world was created, the Father chose not to reveal how long it would last. I cannot tell you when the Son will come again. The Father will send him in his time. Until then, he will exercise patience, for he longs desperately to be with his children in eternity.

Because the Father waits, you have the chance to bring salvation to those who do not yet have hope. Be patient for the Son's coming, and express his love and joy to those around you. The Father will not wait forever, but while he does, you have the chance to introduce his children to him. Eventually, he will decide that it is time for the Son's return. I urge you, though, not to sit and wait for it. Have an active patience—wait, and keep on working.

**Read
2 Peter 3.**

Lord, help me to have your patience, so I might be fruitful while I wait for your Son's return.

*He who is slow to anger is better
than the mighty, and he who
rules his spirit than he who
takes a city.*

—**Proverbs 16:32** (NKJV)

ANGER MANAGEMENT

There are many in the world who believe that the amount of physical power or influence you have proves your strength. That is not the case. Strength is not found in the force of your arms or the force of your personality. True strength is found in your faith in God. If you want to be strong, be like Jesus.

Although Jesus showed anger, his anger was always righteous. He never allowed his anger to get out of control. I can help you rule your spirit in the same way.

Allow me, child, to show you that you can be stronger than your emotions. I made them and I know how they work. With my help you can rule your emotions rather than allowing them to rule you.

**Read
Proverbs 16**.

*Lord, help me to be
strong in you and to
rule my anger.*

A man's discretion makes him slow to anger, and it is his glory to overlook a transgression.

—**Proverbs 19:11** (NASB)

PATIENCE DESPITE OFFENSE

When you are wronged by someone, I know the temptation you face to lash out in response to the affront you have received. Yet being a Christian means following Jesus' example. This means learning to take an insult as an opportunity to show love through patience.

Reply patiently to insults. If possible, overlook the offense altogether. This is no easy task, I realize, but it is important. You do not have to look far to find examples of the destruction that occurs when anger is not held in check. The world is filled with tragedies that could have been avoided had someone exercised patience instead.

Let me help you learn to show love in the midst of an offense. I want you to be above the world, so that your actions and responses will show clearly that you are different because you are a child of God.

Read Proverbs 19.

Help me to be patient when I am wronged, so that I may be an example of Christ.

JULY 11

A ruler can be persuaded through patience, and a gentle tongue can break a bone.

—**Proverbs 25:15** (HCSB)

PEACEFUL PERSUASION

Peace and quiet. How often you admit in the midst of stressful circumstances that you long for a little peace and quiet! I can make peace possible for you today. Simply let go and let me fill you with the spirit of peace. Like fresh air, it will relax your twisted nerves and contentious thoughts.

My peace will prevail. It always does. When you live in my peace, you become less driven and more patient. When you relax your grip on the steering wheel of your life, you allow me room to act.

Patience and peace are companions on life's journey. To have the latter, you must begin to practice the former. I will help you. Just ask.

Read
Proverbs 25:13–20.

I long for the peace that patience makes possible in this hurried world.

LORD, you understand;
remember me and care for me.
Avenge me on my persecutors.
You are long-suffering.

—**Jeremiah 15:15** (NIV)

PATIENCE NEEDED!

In the midst of a trial, Jeremiah needed to be reminded that I am long-suffering. He felt overwhelmed. So do you at times, beloved. While *long-suffering* and *patient* are not typically qualities used to describe God's people, they define me. You can take comfort in knowing that I will carry you through trials. After all, I understand what makes your circumstances so very difficult.

The elasticity of my patience is something on which you can depend. Don't despair, even though some are quick to discredit you or speak unkind things about you. Give that circumstance to me. I will patiently accomplish what needs to happen to bring about the Father's perfect will for your life. My job is to patiently persist. Your job is to patiently trust.

Read
Jeremiah 15:12–18.

My impatience threatens to undermine my faith. I long to be long-suffering, Lord.

JULY 13

Do you show contempt for the riches of his kindness, forbearance and patience, not realizing that God's kindness is intended to lead you to repentance?

—Romans 2:4 (NIV)

PATIENCE TO REPENTANCE

I have patience and mercy for those who belong to the Father. I am patient because I want you to desire to change your behavior. Everyone will be judged after Jesus returns. How you will be judged will depend on your response to my patience and love.

My mercy is new every day. Although the knowledge of my mercy is meant to reassure you, it is not an encouragement to continue in sin. To do so would be, as Paul mentioned, to treat my kindness with contempt.

Though I live within you, your sin nature is still part of you, and it always will be on this side of heaven. But I gladly work within you, helping you avoid the temptation to give in to that nature.

Read
Romans 2:3–4.

I'm sorry, Lord, for the times when I take advantage of your patience. Please forgive and cleanse me.

JULY 14

If we hope for what we do not see, we eagerly wait for it with perseverance.

—**Romans 8:25** (NKJV)

KEEP HOPEFUL

Times are tough. Bills need to be paid, relationships need mending, and sometimes all you want to do is sit and have a good cry. Do that if you feel it helps, but don't lose hope. Always believe that things will get better, because situations will change. Hope is my beautiful creation. It has made leaders out of dreamers and thinkers into doers. I understand that it's difficult—you can't see hope, but it is there. You can trust me—wait for it anyway, knowing that it will happen.

Always remember that I already have everything worked out. Talk to me, tell me what you want, and I will determine if it is for the best. I work things out for your good, but perhaps not how you're expecting.

I know you're hurting and feel lost. But when you pray, I am interceding for you and all will be made right. Maintain your hope—and a little patience.

Read
Romans 8:22–25.

Lord, in the tough times help me to cling to you and to the hope you bring.

We prove ourselves by our purity, our understanding, our patience, our kindness, by the Holy Spirit within us, and by our sincere love.

—**2 Corinthians 6:6** (NLT)

WAIT FOR ME

Beloved, the way I hone a life, sharpen it for my use, isn't always easy or comfortable. As with my servant Paul, I sometimes choose hardship as my tool to sharpen the edges of your faith. Although every event of your life is under my control and timing, you sometimes shy like a horse, doubting my plans and my heart.

I show my love for you by doing the best for you. By exercising patience, you show that you trust me and you prove yourself a loyal and faithful servant.

Do not fear that I am delaying. I am never delayed and I am never late. I am waiting with you. I am always on time with what you need.

Read 2 Corinthians 6:1–7.

Help me to feel your presence and peace while I am waiting for you.

Therefore I, a prisoner for serving the Lord, beg you to lead a life worthy of your calling, for you have been called by God.

—**Ephesians 4:1** (NLT)

A LIFE THAT IS WORTHY

How much are you worth, child? The Father—the Creator of the universe—sent his Son to die for you. That's how much you're worth. Is it any wonder that Paul urged the believers in Ephesus—and now you—to walk in a manner befitting such a high price?

Because of Jesus' death I live within you, guiding you, loving you. You are called to greatness—called to be a servant of the Most High God, to be an ambassador of the kingdom of God. The road of the ambassador for Christ is narrow and difficult at times, while the road of the world is wide and paved with ease. Child, as you walk the difficult road, I am with you as I was with our servant Paul.

Read Ephesians 4:1.

Lord, show me the activities and plans that are worthy of the life to which you have called me.

JULY 17

As God's chosen people, holy and dearly loved, clothe yourselves with compassion, kindness, humility, gentleness and patience.

—**Colossians 3:12** (NIV)

PATIENT WITNESS

Patience is important. Without patience the Father would have destroyed his chosen people when they rebelled. But the Father is slow to anger.

Just as the Father has patience, so can you. Patience stops you from saying things that you will ultimately regret. Patience is part of the fruit I bring to bear in a believer's life.

You are Christ's representative where you are. And as a witness of Christ, I can help you clothe yourself with patience. You must submit to my leading, child. Through patience and a willingness to listen, you will be a more effective witness for Christ. Compassion, kindness, humility, and gentleness are all connected to patience.

Read Colossians 3:5–17.

Lord, slow me down long enough to listen for your leading.

JULY 18

You, however, have followed my teaching, my conduct, my aim in life, my faith, my patience, my love, my steadfastness, my persecutions and sufferings.

—2 Timothy 3:10–11 (ESV)

PATIENCE TO PERSEVERE

Whippings, a shipwreck, stoning, hunger, and thirst are just a few of the hardships Paul faced during his missionary journeys. Through it all Paul endured these trials with patience and perseverance for the sake of Christ.

It is not easy for the Father to allow you to encounter broken relationships, money troubles, pain, or confusion. Yet he will always lead you through these difficulties and allow you to glorify him in the process.

When your journey is tough, don't give up. I will encourage you and give you the strength to persevere for the sake of Christ. I will draw you ever nearer to me through your faithfulness and patience.

Read
2 Timothy 3:10–17.

Lord, sometimes I am so impatient. Help me be patient and trust your plan for me.

JULY 19

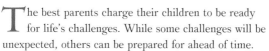

Preach the word; be ready in season and out of season; reprove, rebuke, exhort, with great patience and instruction.

—**2 Timothy 4:2** (NASB)

BE READY

The best parents charge their children to be ready for life's challenges. While some challenges will be unexpected, others can be prepared for ahead of time.

Since Timothy was like a son to Paul, I inspired Paul to prepare Timothy for the challenges of being a leader. Knowing that Jesus' return to earth was imminent, Paul urged Timothy to be ready at a moment's notice to preach the good news or to provide a timely rebuke if needed.

The discipline of readiness is one to which all believers can strive. I can help you be ready at all times to tell of the saving work of Christ in your life. I can also give you the grace and patience to rebuke the wayward and guide those in need of assistance.

Get ready!

Read 2 Timothy 3:10–4:5.

Please help me be on guard for false teachings. Bring me patience to correct and to be corrected.

JULY 20

Jesus said to him, "I do not say to you, up to seven times, but up to seventy times seven."

—**Matthew 18:22** (NASB)

EQUIPPED TO FORGIVE

Child, quit keeping track of how many times a person deserves forgiveness. When Peter asked the Lord how many times he should forgive someone who had sinned against him, the apostle tossed out the number seven as a generous guess. Multiplying Peter's guess exponentially was Jesus' way of showing him the rich abundance of his endless forgiveness.

Breathe me in when you have no forgiveness left to give. Do you feel the strength? My presence in your heart grants you the ability to endure when others have wronged you. It produces long-suffering. Tolerance crowds out offense; patience smoothes over insults. You are able to once again forgive the same person for the same sin multiple times.

Look to me, and I will equip you to forgive others as infinitely as God forgives you.

Read Matthew 18:21–35.

I want to be patient and quick to forgive. Lord, grant me the humility to forgive.

JULY 21

*You have heard of the
perseverance of Job and seen the
end intended by the Lord—that
the Lord is very compassionate
and merciful.*

—**James 5:11** (NKJV)

PATIENCE REWARDED

If anyone can relate to calamity and hardship, it is Job.
Everything good in his life was stolen by the enemy
and he was left with nothing. But Job refused to renounce
his faith and chose instead to endure. It wasn't easy and
he was a hairbreadth away from giving up.

Job's friends offered consolation and advice, but
he still questioned God and pleaded his innocence. He
maintained a mustard-seed-sized kernel of faith and was
ultimately rewarded beyond his loss when he humbly
repented and acknowledged the Lord's omniscience.

Dear one, you have more than a few misguided
friends. But you have me. When Jesus left earth to take
his place of honor and to intercede for you, he sent
me—the Spirit of the Living God—to counsel, lead, and
comfort you. Rely on me through trials, and you will
receive your reward for enduring them.

**Read
James 5:7–18.**

*Lord, give me the
patience of Job and
discernment to know
which voice is your
Spirit.*

JULY 22

Count the patience of our Lord as salvation, just as our beloved brother Paul also wrote to you according to the wisdom given him.

—2 Peter 3:15 (ESV)

YOU'RE WORTH THE WAIT

Beloved, I have heard the frightened whispers of those who fear the judgment to come. Rather than standing firm, generations have given in to a hurried, harried life. But if you're always pushing, peace and patience become pipe dreams.

I want you to reflect on those who have excelled at the task. Consider the perfect patience of Jesus—how he tirelessly trained his disciples, waiting for the fruit of faithfulness to flower within them. For them and for you, I was sent to provide the perseverance to fight the good fight until Jesus' return. The Father waits for you because you are his precious child. And you are worth waiting for. But you need my gift of patience to remain standing while others flee. Don't slip away like a scared disciple. Lean on the grace I provide and soak in the knowledge I have given you in the Word. Most of all, remember: the Father waits.

**Read
2 Peter 3:14–18.**

In my doubt and confusion, you still wait, Lord. Thanks for your precious patience.

JULY 23

The ones that fell on the good ground are those who, having heard the word with a noble and good heart, keep it and bear fruit with patience.

—Luke 8:15 (NKJV)

GROW AND PRODUCE

How I love to watch you grow and blossom! You began with a knowledge of Jesus that was like a seed just planted. Then I watered that seed so that your love for the Savior would develop.

Your soil is rich and you desire to grow. Water your soil by reading my Word and speaking with me, dear one. I want to communicate with you so that I may instruct you on how to mature. Then, when you are ready, you will produce a crop by sharing the wisdom you have received from me. You will help plant seeds of faith in others and help them grow as well.

Do not make your heart hard toward me, but keep it soft, that I might grow in you something more beautiful and fruitful than you could ever imagine.

Read Luke 8:11–15.

Holy Spirit, keep my heart soft toward you. I want to grow and produce fruit for you.

Let us not become weary in doing good, for at the proper time we will reap a harvest if we do not give up.

—**Galatians 6:9** (NIV)

THE GOOD HARVEST

This time of year you are just beginning to enjoy the harvest of fresh produce. Many months of patient work—plowing, planting, fertilizing, weeding—went into bringing the food to your plate.

If the farmer had become too weary to do these things, would there have been anything to harvest? No, his field would be a tangle of weeds.

You tire of doing good things when you aren't getting the recognition you'd like or when the time you are investing isn't showing any benefit or return. Paul reminds you to not grow weary in doing good because at the proper time—my timing, not yours—you will reap a harvest of goodness.

Plant some good seeds today, and watch how I nurture them. Be patient, because in time your harvest will be great.

Read
Galatians 6:7–10.

I promise not to grow impatient doing good, Lord. I look forward to the harvest in your time.

JULY 25

His brothers said to him, "Do you intend to reign over us? Will you actually rule us?" And they hated him all the more because of his dream and what he had said.

—**Genesis 37:8** (NIV)

A LIFE OF PATIENT ENDURANCE

Joseph's life was one of patient endurance. I gave Joseph a dream at a very young age, one that confirmed that he would one day rule over everyone in his family. This didn't sit well with his brothers. They considered murdering him, but they sold him to slave traders instead.

As a slave in Potiphar's house, Joseph was falsely accused and sentenced to prison. While there, I helped him interpret the dreams of Pharaoh's cupbearer and baker. The cupbearer promised to tell Pharaoh about Joseph, but he forgot.

Joseph was released from prison and put into a position of power because I helped him to interpret the pharaoh's dream. His life had taken a decided turn for the better, but still he waited for his first dream to become a reality.

In my timing, Joseph was reunited with, and became ruler of, his family. His patience and faith in me were rewarded. Yours will be too.

**Read
Genesis 37.**

Lord, help me to be as patient as Joseph, to be willing to wait upon your perfect timing.

JULY 26

A dispute also arose among them as to which of them was considered to be greatest.

—**Luke 22:24** (NIV)

GENETIC GREATNESS

Impressionism is more than an artistic style; it is also a Christian's daily responsibility. You are tasked not only with representing the Christian lifestyle but to also give an impression of what God is like. The easiest way to understand this is to realize that when people know you are a Christian, they see your lips move but hear what God would say. On your own it might feel overwhelming to be a loudspeaker for God. Fortunately, that's why he gave you me.

Since you now have me inside you, there is no need to worry about achieving greatness because the greatness I share in God is now a part of you. The same is true for all of your brothers and sisters in Christ. Some families pass on genetic traits like the color of your eyes or hair. God has greatness in his spiritual genes—and through me you have it too.

Read Luke 2:22–35.

Lord, show me your will that I might be an impression of your greatness.

The Lord turned the captivity of Job, when he prayed for his friends: also the Lord gave Job twice as much as he had before.

—**Job 42:10** (KJV)

GOD'S AMAZING AND ABUNDANT BLESSINGS

Can anyone exceed the Lord Almighty in giving? I gave Job twice as much as he had before. Solomon asked for wisdom but was also given great wealth. Abraham prayed for a son and became the father of a nation of descendants numbering the sands of the sea. The disciples asked to share the lunch of a small boy and were given more food than five thousand people could consume.

The lavishness of God's blessings knows no limits. My calling, as the Spirit of the Lord, is to overcompensate those who yield everything to God. Man's imagination cannot begin to comprehend the abundance of blessings a loving and caring God is capable of raining upon his children. And even more abundant will the rewards be in heaven, where mansions are prepared.

Praise God for overflowing treasures!

Read Job 42.

Lord, remind me each day to celebrate the many ways the Spirit rewards me.

JULY 28

*Knowing that the testing of
your faith produces patience.
But let patience have its perfect
work, that you may be perfect
and complete, lacking nothing.*

—James 1:3–4 (NKJV)

TRIALS PERFECT OUR PATIENCE

At one time or another in your life, your plans have
come unraveled. When trials affect your life, you often
cannot see past the here and now to how I can help you.

Dear one, hold on. Even before you pray, things are
moving in the spirit realm. I see what is happening to
you, and this will work out for your edification according
to the Father's plan. Even though you doubt that I am
involved on your behalf, I am quietly at work. Some trials
are longer than others, and they seem overwhelming in
the present. Do not let your perspective be shaped by the
events of today alone. I see your tomorrow, and I have
plans for you.

The patience you are developing through this trial
allows me to use you in even more ways to reach the lost.
Hold on. Help is on the way.

Read
James 1:2–5.

*Lord, remind me that you
are in control during trials.*

JULY 29

See how the farmer waits for the precious fruit of the earth, being patient about it, until it receives the early and the late rains.

—James 5:7 (ESV)

WAIT FOR IT . . .

It can be difficult to work without any guarantee of seeing the fruit of your labor. In fact, all work is based on producing a final product. Many times, doing something solely because it is asked of you can become tiresome and frustrating. Don't worry; the effort you put forth will not be in vain.

After all, because I am within you, any work you do is not done alone. Through my strength, you can accomplish anything asked of you, and together we can produce wonderful fruit.

Sometimes all that is necessary is a little trust and a lot of patience. Believe that the work you have done for God is its own reward, and wait to see what wonderful things grow from it.

Read
James 5:7–8.

Father, help me to trust in you and give me the patience to see your work fulfilled in my life.

JULY 30

*And so, after he had patiently
endured, he obtained the
promise.*

—**Hebrews 6:15** (NKJV)

WAITING ON GOD'S PROMISE

When I made the promise to Abraham that he would be the father of many nations, and that through him all the world would be blessed, he was a man without a home and without children. Even after Abraham faithfully obeyed and left his homeland for Canaan, his family lived as nomads in tents. And the promise of descendants who would one day be as numerous as the stars seemed impossible. Then, when he was one hundred years old and his wife, Sarah, way beyond childbearing years, they had a son.

Abraham had "patiently endured," and so he received what had been promised.

Dear child, though you fear that what you wait for today will never come to fruition, I will help you patiently endure so that in my time and according to my plan, you will receive what I have promised. Count on it.

**Read
Genesis 21:1–7;
Hebrews 6:15.**

*Holy Spirit, as I wait today
for an answer, grant me
the patience to endure as
Abraham did.*

JULY 31

To those who by patience in well doing seek for glory and honor and immortality, he will give eternal life.

—**Romans 2:7** (ESV)

THE PROMISE OF PATIENCE

I know that life can be difficult, dear one. People disappoint you; a promising career path goes awry; you lose the cherished loved one for whom you have prayed diligently. The future that you have been planning for and working hard to achieve can disappear like smoke because of unforeseen circumstances.

At times like these, you are tempted to give up and to lose faith. It is at those times that you must be mindful of patiently persisting in doing what is right, in continuing to pursue excellence in all you do, and in seeking after what brings glory to your Father in heaven. As you strive in obedience to do the will of God, you will be given the greatest gift of all—eternal life.

Whatever you are facing today, remember to be patient, continue to do good, and trust in the result. Your reward is nothing less than heavenly.

Read Romans 2.

Lord, please fill me with your patience that I may continue to do what is right.

AUGUST

THE FRUIT OF THE SPIRIT: KINDNESS

AUGUST 1

The fruit of the Spirit is ... kindness.

—**Galatians 5:22** (NIV)

SAVOR THE FRUIT CALLED KINDNESS

Kindness has a point. I have seen many so-called acts of kindness that were crafted to appear random, yet that wasn't the case at all. When offered only to make a statement or to earn points with the boss, you've wholly missed the mark.

The fruit of kindness that I give you overwhelms, gushes, overflows. It is unexpected, like the gift of grace. It is marked by a heart that is right with the Father. As you receive my kindness, you will feel blessed beyond measure. You will also realize that your motivation to show kindness comes from God.

Superficial kindness is nothing more than sugar-coated disdain. The more upset you are with a person, the more you pretend to care. However, true kindness grows from the seed of love I plant within you because of the Son.

Read
**Galatians 5:16–26;
Colossians 3:12.**

Lord, open my eyes to opportunities you provide for me to show kindness to those in need.

AUGUST 2

Do you despise the riches of His kindness, restraint, and patience, not recognizing that God's kindness is intended to lead you to repentance?

—**Romans 2:4** (HCSB)

GOD'S KINDNESS IN YOU

You see the problems in the world around you. Backbiting, gossip, slander, selfish entitlement, greed, lying—the list of human shortcomings is long, varied, and universal. Even mature Christians are continually sucked into the sin that pulses through humanity.

When you face the temptation to join the din of the sinful chorus, seek to nurture my fruit of kindness instead. Jesus died to crucify those sins that bring such ugliness to the world. He rose to conquer them and sent me to foster the same kindness *in* you that he showed *to* you.

His kindness leads you to gratefulness and repentance. Your kindness to others will have the same effect. There is a very fine line between righteousness and self-righteousness. One leads to life; the other leads to condemnation. Allow me to walk that line with you, leading others to life and repentance through the kindness that flows from me through you.

Read Romans 2:1–4.

Lord, when I am tempted to point out others' sins, humble me to show them your kindness instead of condemnation.

AUGUST 3

Notice how God is both kind and severe. He is severe toward those who disobeyed, but kind to you if you continue to trust in his kindness.

—**Romans 11:22** (NLT)

TRUST IN HIS KINDNESS

Our servant Paul wanted you to understand the two sides of God's nature—he is both kind and severe. His love and kindness are beyond understanding, but he is necessarily severe toward the disobedient. He ruthlessly pursues sin, thoroughly cleanses, and severely prunes so that those who are disobedient might find the truth in him. And, sad to say it, severe punishment awaits those who refuse to acknowledge him. It can be no other way.

To those who trust, however, God is kind. Together, the Father, the Son, and I hear your prayers, draw close to you in times of joy and in times of great need, protecting you, guiding you, comforting you.

So don't be afraid even in the dark times. Trust in our kindness.

Read Romans 11:21–24.

In your mercy, Lord, cleanse my heart from the attitudes that separate me from you.

*God raised us up with Christ
and seated us with him
in the heavenly realms in
Christ Jesus.*

—**Ephesians 2:6** (NIV)

MORE THAN FORGIVENESS

Dear one, the Son's death on the cross was done for more than just forgiveness. It was an expression of love for you. You were burdened by sin, but Jesus pursued you with reckless abandon!

Child, don't ever forget that I share his love for you. When you stumble, my arms surround you and protect you even before you strike the ground. What the Son achieved through the cross is our gift to you. Peace, grace, and the riches of unity with us are all available. Reach out and cling to the Son.

A day is coming when trouble will be no more. The enemy may be hiding it from your eyes, but "the assurance of things hoped for" (Hebrews 11:1 ESV) speaks to the truth. Trust in me, and I will give you a glimpse of the majesty of things to come in the heavenly realms!

**Read
Ephesians 2:1–10.**

*God, grant me an
awareness of my
redemption and identity
in you.*

AUGUST 5

Therefore, as God's chosen people, holy and dearly loved, clothe yourselves with compassion, kindness, humility, gentleness and patience.

—**Colossians 3:12** (NIV)

A GARMENT OF KINDNESS

Beloved, you are one of my chosen ones. I did not call you and come to dwell within you so that you could continue living the way you had been. I called you and now dwell in you in order to help you reflect my love to the world. Love them as I love you.

I'm not expecting you to simply muster up the willpower to be compassionate. In your own strength you cannot love those who persecute you. All I ask is that you offer up yourself as a holy vessel through which I can display my work. I will enable you to put on my compassion and kindness like a garment.

Child, my garment of kindness fits all sizes and situations and is yours for the asking. In this way, all people will know that you belong to me.

Read
Colossians 3:7–17.

Lord, keep me close to you and help me put on your garment of kindness every day. Give me an outpouring of your attributes in my life.

When the kindness of God our Savior and His love for mankind appeared, He saved us.

—**Titus 3:4–5** (HCSB)

GIFT OF KINDNESS

Dear child, I called you from the start. Someone prayed for you, that your heart would be open to my leading. That kindness caused you to seek me. But we must go back even further to see the truth of your salvation.

The kindness and love of the Father and the Son, perfected in the sacrifice for your sins, provided your salvation. God loves his creation—loves *you*—so much that he sent Jesus as the ultimate expression of kindness to others.

His kindness saved you. Nothing you could have done and nothing you will ever do would prove yourself worthy of the sacrifice of the Son. He simply offered you his gift of salvation, and you accepted it.

Now share his kindness with others so they too may experience the ultimate gift of love from the Father and the Son.

Read Titus 3:4–7.

Thank you, Lord, for calling me through your Spirit and for your kind gift of salvation.

AUGUST 7

Now for this very reason also, applying all diligence . . . in your godliness [supply] brotherly kindness, and in your brotherly kindness, love.

—**2 Peter 1:5, 7** (NASB)

RESPOND WITH KINDNESS

As a child of God you make an impression wherever you go. As the fruit of kindness develops in your life, you will walk in a way that is contrary to that of the world.

Sometimes being kind to others isn't easy. When your boss tells you to stop having an office Bible study, when the driver in the next lane cuts you off, when a friend betrays your trust—the world encourages you to take revenge. But don't listen to the world. Listen to me.

Retaliate with kindness. Pray for your boss, smile at the other driver, and love your enemy. In doing these things, you are always in the right! You will never have a reason to apologize when you respond to others with kindness.

The way of the world leads to sin, guilt, and sorrow. The way of the Spirit leads to kindness, freedom, and joy.

**Read
2 Peter 1:1–11.**

Dear Spirit, help me respond with kindness with everyone, whether a friend, stranger, or enemy.

AUGUST 8

You have been so gracious to me and saved my life, and you have shown such great kindness.

—**Genesis 19:19** (NLT)

GREAT KINDNESS

Because of my grace, I sent angels to warn Lot to take his family from Sodom and flee from the coming destruction. He hesitated, but I graciously sent angels to forcibly take Lot and his family by the hand to safety outside the city walls. Even then, as the angels told them to run for their lives and escape to the mountains, Lot still begged for one more favor: to be allowed to flee to a small village instead of to the mountains. I granted his request.

Let his story remind you of the endless grace I offer to all who come to God the Father through faith in the Son. My mercies are new every morning; my kindness is as fresh as the dew on the grass.

I did not turn away from Lot; I will not turn from you.

Read Genesis 19:1–22.

Thank you, Spirit, for your great kindness that you show to me daily.

AUGUST 9

Praise be to the Lord, the God of my master Abraham, who has not abandoned his kindness and faithfulness to my master. As for me, the Lord has led me on the journey to the house of my master's relatives.

—**Genesis 24:27** (NIV)

LEADING BY KINDNESS

Finding a wife for his master's son was not an easy task for Abraham's servant. He had to travel to an unknown land in search of a wife for Isaac, not knowing whether he would succeed. Still, the servant solemnly promised to obey all Abraham's instructions. When he finally arrived at the home of Abraham's family, he stopped and prayed for success and asked me to show kindness to his master, Abraham. As he was still praying, beautiful Rebekah came to the well. When Abraham's servant realized that his prayer had been answered, he fell down in thanksgiving and worshiped God.

Child, I know the tasks in your life that you consider insurmountable. As you come to me in faith and obedience, trusting in me to guide you, I will not withhold my kindness from you. I will lead you to succeed as you allow me to work in you and through you.

Read
Genesis 24.

Lord, do not withhold your kindness from me. Lead me in faithfulness to accomplish your will.

AUGUST 10

Swear to me by the LORD that you will show kindness to my family, because I have shown kindness to you.

—Joshua 2:12 (NIV)

BE KIND

Rahab didn't have to help the spies that Joshua sent out. She could have told the king's soldiers where they were. But she chose to take a risk and be kind to Joshua's men—the enemy of her people. And they spared her life in return.

You too were made to be kind, especially to those whom the world deems unworthy. Jesus communed with lepers, soldiers, the blind, lawyers, beggars, scribes, politicians, priests, tax collectors—all levels of society—sharing the message of redemption. He especially encouraged his followers to show love and kindness to their enemies.

Be a Rahab. Take a risk and be kind. Show people how much they are worth in my eyes.

Read
Joshua 2:8–14.

Sometimes it's hard to be kind. But help me, Lord, to be kind, even when I don't feel like it.

AUGUST 11

May you be blessed of the Lord, my daughter. You have shown your last kindness to be better than the first by not going after young men, whether poor or rich.

—**Ruth 3:10** (NASB)

FILLED WITH KINDNESS

For more than three thousand years, Ruth has inspired those who fear the Lord. I am the One who put it in Ruth's heart to leave her home and family in Moab and to move with her mother-in-law to Bethlehem. Ruth took her cues from Naomi, but she also looked to the God she longed to know. In response, I filled her with kindness.

Beloved, whenever you read in the Scriptures about people acting with kindness toward others, you can be sure that I'm the One making that response possible. I want to give you the means to continue in grace today. Being kind doesn't take wealth, status, or a high IQ. All it takes is a willingness to be available to me and an awareness of others' needs. Let me act through you to fill your world with compassionate deeds today.

Read
Ruth 3:1–13.

In a world of sadness and turmoil, Lord, I'm grateful I can share your kindness with others today.

AUGUST 12

"Don't be afraid," David said to him, "for I will surely show you kindness for the sake of your father Jonathan."

—**2 Samuel 9:7** (NIV)

UNEXPECTED KINDNESS

M ephibosheth had every reason to feel insecure. His grandfather, Saul, had attempted to kill David several times. This man with special needs represented the old administration. Yet I delight in surprising those who have no reason to expect a good outcome. I reminded King David of his close friendship and covenant with Mephibosheth's father, Jonathan. I filled David's heart with kindness. Out of that sprang unexpected hospitality and compassion.

There are broken people in your life who don't expect much. They are afraid of how circumstances might play out in the coming months and years. But I am giving you the same gift I gave Israel's most celebrated king—I am giving you unexpected kindness to share with them. Whether it be at your kitchen table or at the "table of friendship," you have the means to surprise and delight someone today with the kindness I provide.

Read
2 Samuel 9:1–7.

Lord, please show me how to show unexpected kindness toward others in big and little ways.

He who despises his neighbor sins, but happy is he who is gracious to the poor.

—**Proverbs 14:21** (NASB)

SHOWING KINDNESS BRINGS HAPPINESS

No matter where you go, poverty lurks. The poor are the broken, the lost, and the needy. Nonetheless, they too are mine. I enter into their tragedy and despair. I go to them as I go to you: full of grace and mercy.

You can bring my light to them. Will you show kindness to those who usually receive disgust? Will you look beyond the dirty hands and mismatched clothes to the person beneath it all? Do not look away from injustice. Do not flinch when you see the destitute.

I have chosen you to be my voice, hands, and feet to the poor. See them the way I do. Poverty is loneliness, whereas I am friendship. Poverty is lack, but I am fullness. Will you have the courage to see the needy through my eyes and show them my kindness today?

Read Proverbs 14:20–22.

Holy Spirit, please give me your eyes to see the poor and to extend your kindness to them.

Kindness to the poor is a loan to the LORD, and He will give a reward to the lender.

—**Proverbs 19:17** (HCSB)

KINDNESS TO THE POOR

I have always looked upon the leprous, blind, and lame beggars with compassion. I gave the disciples the power to heal bodies as well as hearts. Even now, when I look upon the victims of disease, violence, and poverty, my love is extended to them.

I dwell in all believers and give them my supernatural power to show kindness and help those in need. Child, if you sleep peacefully with a roof over your head, remember those who have no shelter from rain. If you have never known hunger or thirst, think on those who are stricken by famine and drought. Just as you received the gospel so that you may spread it throughout the world, so have you been blessed with material provisions so that you may bless others in need.

When I see you bless the poor with kindness and physical help, I am faithful to bless you with eternal rewards.

**Read
Proverbs 19:1–17.**

Lord, please give me the desire to be kind to the poor.

AUGUST 15

*The islanders showed us
unusual kindness. They built
a fire and welcomed us all
because it was raining and cold.*

—Acts 28:2 (NIV)

UNUSUAL KINDNESS

The Son's kindness bewildered thousands when he
walked the earth. He talked with prostitutes, ate
with drunkards, and embraced the lepers. Outcasts and
untouchables were the center of his attention. I moved the
Son to compassion, and he showed kindness to the lost.
He changed lives through his touch and his words.

The Father is full of compassion, and he uses every
means to show it. It may be through a simple carpenter, a
man of great wealth, islanders who worship foreign gods,
or even a persecutor of the church. He can use you too.

Keep the Father's glory as your focus. Be mindful
of your actions and how they affect those with whom
you interact. Speak with a controlled tongue. Seek the
outcast and those who are downtrodden. Respond with my
benevolence when a person acts against you in anger. Talk
with the desperate, eat with the hurting, and touch those
who seem untouchable.

**Read
Acts 28:1–2.**

*Lord, help me to show
your kindness through
my actions today.*

AUGUST 16

We prove ourselves by our purity, our understanding, our patience, our kindness, by the Holy Spirit within us, and by our sincere love.

—2 Corinthians 6:6 (NLT)

KINDNESS IN ALL CIRCUMSTANCES

Beloved, of all the ways in which you are called to reflect Jesus, there is one in particular that makes you stand out from the world: kindness. In this age of technology, the Internet is used more and more to spread messages that are cruel, demeaning, malicious, and aggressive. Be above this, whatever you do.

As a representative of the Living God, you are called to speak and respond with kindness in all situations. This means that no matter what is said or how it is communicated, you are to show my love through words and acts of kindness.

Nothing will so discredit your ability to share the truth as cruelty. When you fee l tempted to react in an unkind way, pray instead. Ask me to show you how to turn that moment into an opportunity to be a witness for Christ. Show kindness in all circumstances so others can see my sincere love through you.

Read 2 Corinthians 6:1–10.

Please help me to show kindness regardless of the circumstances.

May the Lord reward your work, and your wages be full from the Lord, the God of Israel, under whose wings you have come to seek refuge.

—**Ruth 2:12** (NASB)

GOD-HONORING KINDNESS

Child, I love the risks my people take to honor me. Consider Ruth's circumstances. Leaving Moab and moving to Judah with Naomi was a scary step. Other than her mother-in-law, Ruth knew no one in Bethlehem, but she went anyway. This was an act of great kindness. I knew Ruth's heart and her desire to honor her family and the God of Israel she had come to know.

Her kindness reaped kindness. Hearing of her behavior toward Naomi, Boaz treated Ruth with the kindness she had shown. As a result, both women were provided for and blessed, because Ruth had honored her Lord.

Child, kindness honors me. I stir your heart and provide the means and opportunity to carry out kindness. Honor me today with your caring ways.

Read Ruth 2.

Help me to have the kindness of Ruth in my own life.

AUGUST 18

*They replied, "If you will
be kind to these people and
please them by speaking kind
words to them, they will be
your servants forever."*
—2 Chronicles 10:7 (HCSB)

THE POWER OF KINDNESS

Beloved, a kind act has long-term benefits. Some lives
turn on the pivot of a kind word or deed. Because of
kindness, lives are changed and impact other lives for the
better. Unkindness, on the other hand, is also a pivot that
turns lives, but not for the better.

Wise counselors advised King Rehoboam to act with
kindness toward his subjects. Instead of listening, he chose
to act on the advice of his friends, who advocated harsh
treatment. He reaped the consequences as the nation
divided.

Child, the choice is always yours: to be kind or not.
I will be present to support you in walking in the way of
kindness. I can turn one kind act into that which inspires
millions.

Read
2 Chronicles 10.

*Father, help me to act with
kindness toward others
always.*

AUGUST 19

You, Lord, are good, and ready to forgive, and abundant in lovingkindness to all who call upon You.

—**Psalm 86:5** (NASB)

I WILL LIFT YOU UP

Through good times and bad, David wrote songs for me, and I wrote the song of my love for David in his life.

If your life is harsh, know that it is not because I desire to see you treated harshly. I wish to comfort you during trouble. I am listening to you. Tell me your burdens, and my love will be with you. I am here to save you. If you reach out, we will walk together and I will protect you. Respect my name, and know that I am showing you lovingkindness through my love.

Whenever you are afraid or feel shame, know that I am your refuge. I will lift you up and show my kindness to you. I am good. I am forgiving. My love and my grace never waver. I am reaching out to your soul, and all you need to do is reach back.

Read
Psalm 86.

Lift me into your love today and calm my fear of you.

AUGUST 20

A man who is kind benefits himself, but a cruel man hurts himself.

—**Proverbs 11:17** (ESV)

SIMPLE ACTS

Simple acts of kindness have the power to change the direction of a person's life. Simple acts of kindness can change your life too. If you think back far enough, you will realize the impact that kindness has had on you. Now you have the opportunity to extend such kindness toward others.

It is sometimes hard to be kind, especially to people who hurt you, but kindness is not without rewards. The Son promised, "Love your enemies . . . expecting nothing in return, and your reward will be great" (Luke 6:35 ESV).

I encourage you, dear one, to be kind and gracious to everyone, and trust me for the outcome.

Read
Proverbs 11:13–21.

Heavenly Father, loving those who have hurt me is a challenge greater than I can face without your help. I need you today to love your way.

AUGUST 21

He who oppresses the poor reproaches his Maker, but he who honors Him has mercy on the needy.

—**Proverbs 14:31** (NKJV)

HONOR THE NEEDY

People try to demean those who are less fortunate, but all people—even those who are destitute—are valuable and precious in God's eyes. You honor the Father when you show mercy to the needy.

You encounter people in need every day—the homeless veteran holding a cardboard sign, the teenage mother quieting her child, the father eating at the soup kitchen, the lonely widow. When you see them, you feel uneasiness in your stomach because I am working in you. I tug at your soul for a reason. Act. Show them compassion and mercy.

You may not know what to do, but rely on me, and I will show you what to do.

Read
Proverbs 14:20–31.

Lord God, grant me the humility to open my heart to those in need.

AUGUST 22

So the LORD spoke kind and comforting words to the angel who talked with me.

—**Zechariah 1:13** (NIV)

HE WILL LISTEN AND RESTORE

When Zechariah pleaded on behalf of the nation of Judah, I listened. While my righteous wrath was ignited by their rebellion and they suffered the consequences for their sin, I was moved with compassion for their suffering. They learned the hard way that I demand wholehearted commitment and faithfulness.

Still, I always do what is best for you and help you make the right choices. Even when you are being disciplined, we always have a plan to restore you.

Dear one, never be ashamed to confess your wrongs to me. Don't cower in fear, believing that I will refuse to listen. Instead, call out to me. I will guide you back to the Father and speak words of kindness and comfort that will restore you.

**Read
Zechariah 1:12–17.**

Thank you, Lord, for being a compassionate and caring God.

AUGUST 23

Love is patient, love is kind. It does not envy, it does not boast, it is not proud.

—**1 Corinthians 13:4** (NIV)

WHAT LOVE REALLY IS

Child, love is not easy, quick, or cruel. It never leads you to compromise your principles or disobey the Father's will for your life. It does not come with conditions or demands to "prove" your love by acts that dishonor God or yourself. Love led a Savior to the cross, to suffer and die for those he loved. Beloved child, *this* is love.

As you become more like Christ, the fruit of love for others will flow. I am here to open your eyes and heart to those who desperately need kindness. I will help you put aside your selfish desires and reach out to others.

Dear one, there are people in your life who are not always easy to love. But they need to know the Savior's love for them. What great joy the Father has in seeing you love others the way he loves you!

Read 1 Corinthians 13.

Open my eyes to the people around me that need kindness. Please help me put aside my selfish ways and be kind to others.

*Be kind to one another,
tenderhearted, forgiving
one another, even as God in
Christ forgave you.*

—**Ephesians 4:32** (NKJV)

FORGIVENESS IS KEY

I know that forgiving others can be a hard thing for you to do. But I am here to help you. I know what betrayal and rejection feel like. I still love abundantly though my people have rejected me many times. Likewise, you can be willing to forgive for my sake.

Though the church is one body in Christ, this is not a guarantee that everyone will always get along. I can help all believers love one another.

Just as the Father forgave you in the Son's death, you must forgive others. I will not leave you to forgive in your own strength. Allow me to give you the grace you need. Forgiveness is the key to a healthy church.

Read
Ephesians 4:25–32.

*Holy Spirit, help me
remember the forgiveness
you give me and pass it on
to others.*

AUGUST 25

Encourage the young women to love their husbands and to love their children.

—**Titus 2:4** (HCSB)

REACH FOR KINDNESS

As you manage your home or office today, what will you take from the cupboards, cabinets, or desk drawers? Have you thought about taking the fruit of my kindness and love—the art of being able to smile as you lug the loads of laundry to the washer, fix yet another meal, or deal with frustrating coworkers—to others? What a gift kindness would be in your home, school, or workplace.

You can have that gift. A basket of kindness and love awaits you. Go ahead, reach for it. The fruit is ripe, but not too ripe. Not too soft, not too firm. Not too bitter, not too sweet. Just perfect. And waiting for you.

Have I enticed you enough yet? Come, do what is good. Reach for and take the fruit of kindness I'm offering you. It really is delicious. And then offer the basket of the fruit of kindness to others.

Read Titus 2:3–5.

Father, help me show love and kindness to others today, even when I don't feel like it.

*Be kind, always showing
gentleness to all people.*

—**Titus 3:2** (HCSB)

CONTINUALLY KIND

Beloved, I sense your defensiveness at the command
to speak no evil and to be gentle and meek. *Do you
know how hard it is to work with her? Isn't meekness a
sign of weakness? It's all about survival in this dog-eat-dog
world!* Oh how I understand, precious child.

My spirit of kindness dwelling in you allows you to
pour out kindness to others, even and especially when
they do not deserve it. It is not about what they do or
don't deserve. It's about what is expected of *you*, the very
one I've been sent to fill and guide into righteousness.

Continually relying on me to manifest the fruit of
kindness by no means makes you weak. Which requires
more strength: to rant about someone or to talk to her
and help her try to understand the reasons behind her
behavior? My power helps you choose the latter. Kindness
will set you apart.

Read
Titus 3:1–8.

*Holy Spirit, help me to
replace bitter or even
physical defensiveness with
your perfect kindness.*

*Deal well with me, O Sovereign
LORD, for the sake of your own
reputation! Rescue me because
you are so faithful and good.*

—**Psalm 109:21** (NLT)

MY LOVINGKINDNESS

A s the Spirit of God, you have known me as your
rescuer in various stages throughout your life. I have
also saved you from dangers and harm that you remain
unaware of, such as when I sent you on a detour when
danger lurked ahead. You are mine, and I take care of
you.

Goodness is my essence, because I am love. I desire
the best for you and set perimeters to protect you from
the evil powers of this harsh world. Though you may feel
helpless, hemmed in, or oppressed by circumstances or
people, my faithfulness and goodness are your refuge.

My love is unfailing and I deal with you kindly. I
want good *for* you so that I can work good *through* you
for my name's sake. Let me lavish you with my kindness.

**Read
Psalm 109:20–31.**

*Spirit, may I be a willing
vessel to receive your
lovingkindness and then
pour it out to others.*

AUGUST 28

The next day we landed at Sidon; and Julius, in kindness to Paul, allowed him to go to his friends so they might provide for his needs.

—**Acts 27:3** (NIV)

I PROVIDE

Paul had just gone through a terrible ordeal before Festus and Agrippa. He stood strong and did not waver, knowing that I would provide for him no matter what the outcome would be. He was sent to Rome to bear testimony to Caesar.

My servant did well, and I showed my compassion to him. Before his great journey, I allowed him a time of rest. I provided a way for him to fellowship with some of my followers.

I always care for my followers. Those who place their hope in me are given rest. In a time of great hardship, beloved, trust that I will give you rest. Though following my leading will not be easy, I can promise peace in your heart. Come to me and find rest from the trials of life.

Read Acts 27:1–4.

Spirit divine, give me the strength to endure the hard days and trust that you will care for me.

But as for you, you meant evil against me; but God meant it for good.

—Genesis 50:20 (NKJV)

THE KINDNESS CORPS

It is turning out to be one of the worst days you have ever spent at work. Your boss came in and yelled at you, several coworkers laughed at you, and to top it all off, a woman behind you in line at the store is now yelling at you. It would be really easy to return insult for insult. Except you've been recruited by God, and now you're part of the Kindness Corps.

It's time to counter that anger, malice, and mean-spiritedness with love, tenderness, and yes, kindness. And when it seems impossible, well, I can help you with that. While I can't make you say the right words, I can encourage you to step aside and let her go in front of you. I can give you the words to say, but you'll have to say them. Together our greatest weapon is kindness.

Read Genesis 50:15–21.

Lord, help me to show kindness, especially when I don't want to.

AUGUST 30

Evil-merodach ascended to the Babylonian throne. He was kind to Jehoiachin and released him from prison.

—**Jeremiah 52:31** (NLT)

DISPLAYING DEEDS OF KINDNESS

In a world of greed, selfishness, and narcissism, deeds of kindness are almost incomprehensible. That an enemy king could show kindness to the king of Judah is evidence of my work. That Joseph—who had risen to a position of authority and power—could forgive his brothers for selling him into slavery, and then grant them vast provisions, is evidence of my spirit of kindness within him.

No act of grace, however, will ever eclipse the sacrifice Christ made in giving his own life for an undeserving, unappreciative, ungrateful world. His decision to take on the sins of all people was a choice motivated by a love so profound, it will forever remain unfathomable. It is only fitting that you should do your best to reflect his love by also performing acts of unmitigated kindness.

Read Jeremiah 52:31–33.

Holy Spirit, grant me the desire to show your mercy by deeds of kindness.

AUGUST 31

Let the young woman to whom I shall say, "Please let down your jar that I may drink," and who shall say, "Drink, and I will water your camels"—let her be the one whom you have appointed for your servant Isaac. —**Genesis 24:14** (ESV)

IT'S A SIGN

People tend to look for signs everywhere, especially in romantic relationships. The same questions begin to bounce around in your head from date to date: "Is he the one?" "Can I put up with the way she plays with her hair or bites her nails?" "Do we have enough in common?" But after the dates, the questioning, and the final realization that the answer is *yes* to all of those questions, there's still something you've been waiting for . . . God's okay.

Hopefully you'll listen to me when I start nudging you toward others. Kindness is the best foundation for both genuine friendships and lifelong relationships.

Read Genesis 24:12–19.

God, give me your guidance in all my relationships that I might treat others the way you would.

SEPTEMBER
THE FRUIT OF THE SPIRIT: Goodness

SEPTEMBER 1

The fruit of the Spirit is . . .
goodness.

—**Galatians 5:22** (NASB)

SAVOR THE FRUIT CALLED GOODNESS

I love the way you are drawn to my fruit called goodness and try diligently to avoid its opposite. This fruit counters darkness. The negativity abounding in this broken world makes seeing the good very difficult. I know at times you are frustrated because those who should be filled to the brim with God's goodness falter or fall.

If you look solely at the goodness that the world tries to give, you will see only a smeared, dark window. So think instead of the Son's goodness and picture a spotless skylight, clean and shining.

Rejoice when you see such goodness in a child, neighbor, or spouse. But don't despair when you see examples of the opposite. Goodness grows best when nurtured. I can help you plant its seeds in those around you as you live true to your faith.

Read
Galatians 5:16–26;
2 Thessalonians
1:11.

Heavenly Father, show me simple ways to daily share gifts of goodness with others.

SEPTEMBER 2

*Surely goodness and mercy
shall follow me all the days of
my life, and I shall dwell in
the house of the LORD forever.*

—**Psalm 23:6** (ESV)

HOPE FOR THE FUTURE

Child, do not worry when the burdens of this world grow heavy. There will be difficult times, but you have nothing to fear. I'm not going anywhere. The Son and the apostles told you again and again that nothing could separate you from my love. I am good to those I love, dear one.

This life is temporary, and infinitely better days are coming. Cherish this opportunity to love and encourage others in light of the goodness and mercy to come. You are called to preach the gospel through your words and deeds. When I call you home, it will be with joy, not fear. It is my desire that your joy be without regrets, not in spite of them.

Live according to my will. Walk according to my ways, not out of obligation, but in love. Everything I desire is for your benefit.

**Read
Psalm 23.**

*Lord, give me your strength,
so that I can live a life that
honors you daily.*

SEPTEMBER 3

We know that all things work together for good to those who love God, to those who are the called according to His purpose.

—**Romans 8:28** (NKJV)

REDEMPTION THROUGH LOVE

I called you out of darkness, dear one. Christ rescued you when you were still engulfed in sin. You were shown mercy when you were perishing; will I now withhold grace and goodness from the redeemed?

Not everything will be pleasant. I am refining you through trials, but you can trust that my will is for your benefit. You are made in our divine image, and through our love and careful crafting, you are growing in righteousness.

I know the most hidden parts of your soul, and I will not give you more than you can bear. When challenges come, take your focus off your circumstances and turn your gaze to me. Be thankful that I have chosen you to glorify the Lord!

**Read
Romans 8:23–35.**

Lord, give me the patience to endure trials and the wisdom to see your purpose behind it.

SEPTEMBER 4

I myself am satisfied about you, my brothers, that you yourselves are full of goodness, filled with all knowledge and able to instruct one another.

—**Romans 15:14** (ESV)

A LIVING EXAMPLE OF GOODNESS

When you became a Christian, you gained an understanding of the goodness of God, and by this understanding you are able to share that goodness with others. By following my promptings and living out the Word with integrity, you become a vibrant example of Christ in this world. In this way, you are able to be not only a light to those who are lost but also an encouragement and support to your brothers and sisters in Christ.

Do not underestimate how much you need one another. Without godly company to fortify you, it is easy to fall away from me and into the patterns of the world. But those who strengthen one another are likely to increase in goodness as well.

Strive for this. This is the path I want you to take; it is the path that pleases me. It is not an easy path. You will need my help every day to live out goodness in this dark and fallen world. Because I am with you, you need only to ask.

**Read
Romans 15:13–19.**

May I honor you today, Lord, as I strive to live out your goodness.

*Walk as children of light
(for the fruit of the Spirit is in
all goodness, righteousness, and
truth).*

—**Ephesians 5:8–9** (NKJV)

A CHILD OF LIGHT

Child, many consider themselves to be good people.
But true goodness comes from me. It is the condition
of your heart, a condition that overflows in action.

Jesus modeled how you should live. I help you to
follow his example. Though I help, I cannot do it for you.
Your goal must be to imitate the goodness of Christ—to
walk as a child of light.

Doing good only on the outside is not what I care
about. I want you to be filled with goodness that overflows
to others. Seek me, learn from me, and allow me to align
your heart with mine. When your heart is aligned with
mine, you will live out my fruit of goodness.

Read
Ephesians 5:1–10.

*Teach my heart to be
like yours, to want what
you want and to feel how
you feel.*

SEPTEMBER 6

And have tasted the goodness of the word of God and the powers of the age to come.

—**Hebrews 6:5** (ESV)

CHOOSE GOODNESS

Beloved child, I realize people make mistakes. Some people in the early church made a grievous choice. They had experienced the goodness of the gospel and my indwelling presence. They had known the very goodness that comes from the Word, the power of the age to come; yet they chose to chase after worthless idols that had no power to satisfy or save.

I also know that each day you are confronted by many different voices. Some promise you financial reward if only you would compromise your integrity. Others hold out the allure of popularity and success if you would turn your back on your beliefs. You too have tasted the goodness of the Word of God. You have shared in my presence. So as a true believer and through the power of my indwelling spirit, hold fast to God and his Word, no matter how strong the pull to walk away. A heavenly reward is assured for all who persevere.

Read Hebrews 6:1–12.

Spirit, keep before me today the goodness of God and his Word, and help me to hold fast.

SEPTEMBER 7

*Like newborn infants, desire
the pure spiritual milk, so that
you may grow by it for your
salvation, since you have tasted
that the Lord is good.*

—1 Peter 2:2–3 (HCSB)

GROW IN GOODNESS

Beloved, the goal of a parent is for a child to grow into
maturity, not only physically but in all aspects of
life. Nothing grieves a parent more than to watch a child
who has been given every opportunity to succeed, struggle
and fail to achieve his or her potential. The child remains
stuck in immaturity, hindered in their development. The
same is true of God's children. I want you to realize the
vast extent of his goodness to you and the rich spiritual
nourishment that comes from living in Christ. I will help
instill your desire to keep growing.

Child, consider your appetite for the sustenance that
comes from the Word. I am with you to strengthen and
feed you as you seek to grow in faith. Taste the fruit of
my goodness today. You will not be disappointed.

**Read
1 Peter 2:1–10.**

*Thank you, Lord, for the
goodness of the Word. Fill
me with a desire to be fed
and grow.*

SEPTEMBER 8

His divine power has given to us all things that pertain to life and godliness, through the knowledge of Him who called us by glory and virtue.

—2 Peter 1:3 (NKJV)

HE PROVIDES

I've heard the lies of those who claim to speak for me, those who boast of secret knowledge that I haven't provided them. They speak of ways to reach God, yet these paths lead only to destruction. They may have famous people in their ranks, they may have a lot of money and influence, but they are teaching only lies.

Don't overwhelm yourself with the notion of what you have to do to bring honor to the Father. I will gladly provide all that you need to grow in grace and wisdom and in the knowledge of Jesus. You will lack for nothing. Just trust me to work in you and through you.

When you feel inadequate to the task, trust in my adequacy and sufficiency.

Read
2 Peter 1:3–11.

Heavenly Father, thank you for the Spirit's guidance.

SEPTEMBER 9

For this very reason, make every effort to supplement your faith with goodness, [and] goodness with knowledge.

—2 Peter 1:5 (HCSB)

SPIRITUAL HEALTH

Many people take vitamin supplements to maintain good health. They ingest calcium, nutrients, iron, and fiber, hoping to stimulate their physical well-being. Beloved, there is nothing wrong with taking vitamins. But do not neglect to supplement your spirit with faith and goodness. Do not forget that I provide mental, emotional, and spiritual peace, satisfaction, growth, strength, and endurance. The health I provide transcends the clay that temporarily encases the human soul.

Make time with me part of your daily regimen. Submit to the ways I help you exercise your faith through characteristics like the goodness and knowledge of Jesus. Let me nourish your soul so that your strength will be renewed each morning.

Read
2 Peter 1:5.

Righteous Spirit, build spiritual muscle within me as I spend time with you.

SEPTEMBER 10

*I will make all My goodness
pass before you, and I will
proclaim the name of the LORD
before you. I will be gracious
to whom I will be gracious,
and I will have compassion on
whom I will have compassion.*

—**Exodus 33:19** (NKJV)

OH MY GOODNESS!

Remember when the rich young ruler called Jesus
"Good Teacher"? The Savior replied, "No one
is good but One, that is, God" (Mark 10:17–18 NKJV).
The Son of God was referring to me. I am the Spirit of
goodness. Those I touch do good things. Where I go,
goodness follows. And that is what occurred that day in
the Sinai wilderness. Moses had been assured that he
would not be alone as he continued to lead the Israelites
to the Promised Land. But the weary leader needed a
tangible reminder that God would make good on the
promise to go with him. That's where I stepped in. I gave
Moses a peek at my gracious nature.

If you will quiet yourself and read the Scriptures with
an open heart, you will see my determination to make
good on my promises. You will see how much I long to be
gracious. Isn't that good news?

**Read
Exodus 33:14–23.**

*Like Moses, I have seen
tangible reminders of your
goodness and love.*

SEPTEMBER 11

Perhaps the LORD will see my affliction and restore goodness to me instead of Shimei's curses today.

—2 Samuel 16:12 (HCSB)

HE FEELS YOUR PAIN

King David's son Absalom had stolen his father's throne and carried out a coup. The maligned monarch was a fugitive. As he fled for his life, he was pummeled with stones. But David didn't retaliate. Instead, he trusted the Lord for a good outcome. This poet and king knew me and my nature. He held out for what he was convinced would not be long in coming—the Lord's goodness.

Beloved, I know how much it hurts to be mocked. Being falsely accused fuels resentment. I can sense your despair when you are treated wrongly. Oh, how I ache when you ache. But can you feel the warmth of my presence? I am here with you, to help you stand when you feel like crumpling. Come to me with your deepest need.

Read 2 Samuel 16:5–14.

Lord, my pain is bearable as long as I know that your goodness will sustain me.

SEPTEMBER 12

They blessed the king and went to their homes joyful and glad of heart for all the goodness that the LORD had shown.

—1 Kings 8:66 (ESV)

THE PEOPLE REJOICE OVER GOD'S GOODNESS

Solomon spent weeks offering sacrifices to the Almighty and having his people continuously praise Yahweh for his abundant blessings. Job began his day with prayers and sacrifices to the Lord. Daniel started each morning by turning to the east and lifting his prayers to God.

I, the Spirit of gratitude and rejoicing, am pleased when righteous hearts joyfully acknowledge the wonder of being aligned with God. To serve the Lord cheerfully and to receive his overflowing blessings in return is a harmony ordained by me. I give you cause each day to celebrate God's love, protection, grace, and provision.

"Praise the LORD! Praise, O servants of the LORD, praise the name of the LORD!" (Psalm 113:1 ESV).

Read
1 Kings 8:54–66.

Help me, Lord, to continuously celebrate your goodness.

Our ancestors ... ate until they were full and grew fat and enjoyed themselves in all your blessings.

—**Nehemiah 9:25** (NLT)

THE PEOPLE DELIGHT IN GOD'S GOODNESS

There is no shame regarding success in life if your prosperity has been arrived at through honest dealings and diligent labor. Abraham's flocks were vast; Job's fields were bountiful; Solomon's palaces were massive and ornate. Those who meditate day and night on the Word of God learn that I, the Spirit of judgment, deem them to be wise, and I often make them prosperous and successful. My rewards are limitless. My grace is lavish. My bounty is immense.

Nehemiah blessed the Lord with his remembrance of God's goodness. You are called to be a person who delights in serving the Lord, reading his Word, obeying his commands, and praising his name. When you are such a person, you will be rewarded in grand measure, perhaps in tangible wealth but certainly in spiritual rewards.

Read Nehemiah 9:21–25.

Holy Spirit, I unite with you in joyous praise of a bountiful God.

SEPTEMBER 14

Surely your goodness and love will follow me all the days of my life, and I will dwell in the house of the LORD forever.

—**Psalm 23:6** (NIV)

GOD'S GOODNESS PURSUES

Beloved, I know your deep desires, how you long to be pursued. Pursuit is the mark of ardent love. Even those who love the chase also long to be chased.

Child, I know every hair, every thought, and every dream you have. I loved you from the very beginning and will continue to love you for all eternity. My love for you is active, not passive. I pursue you into darkness in order to bring you back to the light. I go where you go. My goodness will follow you all the days of your life here and in eternity.

When this world ends, you will join the King of kings in the place he has prepared for you. And what joy will follow!

Read Psalm 23:4–6.

Lord, thank you for your love and the reminder that you have prepared a place for me.

SEPTEMBER 15

*He has granted to us his precious
and very great promises.*

—2 Peter 1:4 (ESV)

CLING TO THE PROMISES

Knowing the love God has for you and understanding
why Christ died for you will give your life meaning.
Now you can live a life that glorifies him. You are not
in the hopeless state you once were. You can be hopeful,
beloved, because I am faithful to keep my promises.

You have the promise of my indwelling, child. I will
never leave you. Because I dwell within you, I guide you
and go with you wherever my lead takes you. I am leading
you home toward heaven, to dwell forever with Jesus.
You also have the promise of my love, which can never be
taken away from you.

You are precious to me. Hold fast to my promises.

**Read
2 Peter 1:4.**

*Lord, I sometimes forget to
cling to the most basic of
your promises: the promise
of your constant presence.
When I am afraid, comfort
me with this promise.*

SEPTEMBER 16

According to His mercy He saved us, through the washing of regeneration and renewing of the Holy Spirit.

—Titus 3:5–6 (NKJV)

THE GOODNESS OF SALVATION

You are loved as if you were the only child of God. When you were lost in darkness, Jesus found you. When sin entangled you, the Son set you free, gladly paying the terrible price you were unable to pay. It was worth the sacrifice, dear one, not because of anything you had done, but because the Father's deepest desire was to call you his child.

In your helplessness and fear, I was sent to provide aid. You were filthy in your sins, but I have cleansed you of every speck of dirt. Now I can give you abundant life on earth and eternal life in heaven. Through me, you will have peace and joy for the present. In me, you will find hope for the future.

What greater gift can there be than that of your salvation?

Read Titus 3:3–8.

Spirit Divine, thank you for your goodness and your salvation.

SEPTEMBER 17

*With this in mind, we constantly
pray for you, that our God . . .
may bring to fruition your every
desire for goodness.*

—**2 Thessalonians 1:11** (NIV)

A DESIRE FOR GOODNESS

The disciples understood that it was the Father who
brought thousands to salvation, rather than their
actions. The disciples desired goodness and walked by
faith, and God blessed their deeds. He brought forth fruit
because they followed my promptings and focused on
heavenly things.

Many people wander through their lives alone,
looking to their own strength to bring things to fruition.
Sometimes their efforts fail and they lose sight of their
blessings. Sometimes their efforts succeed and they keep
the glory for themselves. Yet good cannot happen apart
from God.

My goodness is never absent when your life darkens.
Long to glorify God and I will honor your desire for
goodness.

Read
2 Thessalonians
1:11–12.

*I desire your goodness,
Lord, so your glory may
be evident in my life.*

*You were once darkness, but
now you are light in the Lord.
Live as children of light.*

—**Ephesians 5:8** (NIV)

CHILDREN OF LIGHT

On the first day of creation, the word was spoken. Immediately, there was light and it illuminated the universe. The light was good.

You should not be surprised to be described as a light in the Lord. Light scatters darkness, makes the path visible, and allows others to see the truth.

Evil does its deeds in the dark. When the light of goodness, righteousness, and truth appears, evil is exposed. How wonderful to be a bearer of the light to a dark world, a bringer of truth to a world trapped by lies.

You were once in that darkness; someone cared enough to shine the truth into your life. Now you are to bring the light to others who need the goodness of the Lord.

Read
Ephesians 5:8–20.

*Thank you, Jesus, for
bringing me out of the
darkness and into the light.*

SEPTEMBER 19

*The Israelites will return and
seek the LORD their God....
They will come trembling to the
LORD and to his blessings in the
last days.*

—**Hosea 3:5** (NIV)

COME CLOSER

Child, have you noticed that you've distanced yourself
from me? That you are spending less time with
me and more time with the world? Losing your devotion
saddens me. Do you hear me calling you to return to the
intimacy we once shared?

The goodness of the Lord awaits you. You were
bought with a price—Jesus made the ultimate sacrifice for
your redemption. Come and experience the goodness of
the Lord that has been set aside just for you.

Place the Lord first in your life, then others—your
family, your neighbors, your friends—and lastly, yourself.
He has commanded you to love him with all of your heart,
soul, mind, and strength.

Come closer and enjoy the blessings of the Lord's
abiding goodness.

**Read
Hosea 3:1–5.**

*I am prone to wander,
Lord. Bring me back to
your goodness.*

SEPTEMBER 20

"I will satisfy the priests with abundance, and my people will be filled with my bounty," declares the LORD.

—**Jeremiah 31:14** (NIV)

SATISFACTION IN GOD

You are truly loved, child. It is my good pleasure to provide what you need. But I know that, because of your fallen nature, you will want more. You need to learn to be content with what you've been given. You need to find your satisfaction in heavenly things, not earthly things. This is why Jesus encourages you to avoid storing up treasure on earth.

You are designed to be eternally satisfied only by a relationship with your Creator. Have faith in Jesus. You are the Son's witnesses on earth—and just as the Father supplied for the priests of Israel, so he will take care of you.

Read Jeremiah 31:10–14.

I choose, Lord, to find my satisfaction in you.

SEPTEMBER 21

They shall come and sing in the height of Zion, and shall flow together to the goodness of the LORD . . . and they shall not sorrow any more at all.

—**Jeremiah 31:12** (KJV)

RETURN TO ME

When the children of Israel were exiled, I spoke to them through prophets like Jeremiah, giving them my promise to restore them to their land. In their sin they were captured. In their repentance they were delivered. So it is with you, dear one. Whenever fear, doubt, or other reasons cause you to turn away from me, I wait for you with open arms to return.

Child, because you were ransomed by the Savior, you may rest assured that I can cultivate your soul as never before. I promise you the constancy of my presence, especially when you face hardships. I will always be with you to guide you. I will show you which path you should take. Sincerely seek me, and you will find me.

In returning, your soul will find the rest it desires.

Read Jeremiah 31:10–14.

Holy Spirit, help me to see that you are waiting for me.

SEPTEMBER 22

*Your people settled in it, and
from your bounty, God, you
provided for the poor.*

—**Psalm 68:10** (NIV)

I FILL AND FULFILL

You have needs, and I am the Provider. All who are in God's family are under my providence. Those who are poor will have their lives filled by me. I bring fulfillment and purpose for each member. None are excluded. I sustain them all.

If you need something, I will provide it for you. There is no waste in my providence, but there is the excess of an overflowing cup. It is my joy to give to anyone who calls upon my name.

As I renew lives, I restore to glory what was once lost. Everything that I give is free—my gift to you. If you accept it, you will find fulfillment. Those who come to me and dwell under my protection are safe.

**Read
Psalm 68:1–10.**

*Help me believe. Show me
that you care enough to
provide what I need.*

SEPTEMBER 23

He fills my life with good things. My youth is renewed like the eagle's!

—**Psalm 103:5** (NLT)

YOU ARE BLESSED

How blessed you are, dear one! Your heavenly Father has adopted you as one of his own children, so now you can take part in all of his blessings. And I am a guarantee that there are more good things to come.

King David sang of my goodness. Will you do likewise? Each day I fill your life with a cornucopia of goodness and blessings. I am here to provide all that you need, whether through a friend's listening ear, a timely word of advice, or a meal delivered to you.

There may be circumstances where it is difficult to see the good. Do not be discouraged! I will restore you and strengthen you.

Get ready to soar like an eagle.

Read Psalm 103.

Thank you for adopting me as your own. Help me rely on your promise of goodness for my life.

SEPTEMBER 24

But You, O G<small>OD</small>, the Lord, deal kindly with me for Your name's sake; because Your lovingkindness is good, deliver me.

—**Psalm 109:21** (NASB)

MEANT FOR GOOD

King David cried out to the Lord in his suffering. Yet he came in faith, wholeheartedly believing in the lovingkindness of God. Such a prayer always blesses us.

Child, consider how you approach the Father. Sometimes you come in faith that God hears and cares. More often you cringe before his throne, unsure of your welcome.

Beloved of God, know that the Father always is good, always is kind. Out of kindness I was sent to comfort and to provide. In each circumstance, I am wholeheartedly at work for good in your life.

Dear one, I know your suffering. When you suffer, I suffer. Believe that I am good and that you are heard and loved.

Read Psalm 109.

Please help me to trust that things will work out for good. May I walk in your promise today.

They celebrate your abundant goodness and joyfully sing of your righteousness.

—**Psalm 145:7** (NIV)

SING YOUR OWN WAY

I am intimately aware of what causes spontaneous praise to burst forth from your lips. When your heart is full to overflowing, you long to proclaim your joy to anyone with ears to listen.

I inspired David to praise the work of the Lord, to proclaim the Father's greatness. Further inspiration came from meditating on the Scriptures—feasting on the Father's faithfulness to his people over generations. My inspiration set David's will in motion, making him determined to praise. Now his praise helps feed your soul.

Sing, child. In your own way, sing of the greatness of the Father and the grace of the Son. It is my great pleasure to celebrate with you.

Read Psalm 145.

Dear Father, encourage me to testify of your goodness to others so that all may praise you.

SEPTEMBER 26

*Let Your priests, O LORD God,
be clothed with salvation,
and let Your saints rejoice in
goodness.*

—**2 Chronicles 6:41** (NKJV)

AN INVITATION

Solomon's prayer pleased me. It always fills me with joy to know that my loved ones want to be with me, speak with me, and be filled by me. Solomon asked me for assistance and gave me blessing and praise. He asked me to come and be with him. He invited my power to rest on him and his people. I gladly do this for anyone who asks. I give to those who seek wisdom, strength, and courage.

You can learn from this prayer. Take it into your heart and learn from Solomon's wisdom. Speak to me, your guide and mentor, often. Tell me what is on your heart and mind. Ask of me what you need. Just as Solomon came to me for my blessing and assistance, ask when you have need. I will give to you gladly.

**Read
2 Chronicles
6:39–42.**

*Spirit, help me remember
to speak to you and ask for
your help. I can do nothing
by myself.*

SEPTEMBER 27

*They sang responsively, praising
and giving thanks to the LORD,
"For he is good, for his steadfast
love endures forever toward
Israel."*

—Ezra 3:11 (ESV)

MORE THAN GOOD ENOUGH

Child, you bring such joy to me when your gratitude and praise overflow in worship. I thrill at your undivided attention and devotion. With complete surrender and adoration, you and I are unified. Because I inhabit the praises of God's people, you and I commune and celebrate as one when you praise and worship him in spirit and in truth.

But the full truth is that sometimes that place of sweet union is difficult to find. Gratitude dries up or distractions hinder focus. Self-condemnation sets in as you view your humanity as unworthy of such joy.

I do not condemn you for being human, precious one, and I make myself available to help you overcome feelings of inadequacy or failure. When you feel you are not good enough to be in the Lord's presence, always remember that my infinite goodness is enough for both of us.

**Read
Ezra 3:7–11.**

*You are so good, Lord!
Thank you for goodness
that covers me in your
grace and steadfast love.*

*Learn to do right; seek justice.
Defend the oppressed. Take
up the cause of the fatherless;
plead the case of the widow.*

—**Isaiah 1:17** (NIV)

FOLLOW MY LEAD

On the eve of Jesus' betrayal he told the disciples, "When he, the Spirit of truth, comes, he will guide you into all the truth" (John 16:13 NIV). Jesus knew his followers would need direction, and he sent me to provide it.

Trust me to instruct you in the ways of righteousness. I will teach you to love justice and to pursue it for those who cannot. I will equip you to help the helpless and to stand in the gap for those who have been taken advantage of or abandoned. You will console the lonely and comfort the brokenhearted. You will spread the love of the Father because of me and because I get my direction from him.

Look for my promptings and feel my nudges. Your sense of discernment develops as our relationship strengthens. I am guiding you now. Follow and I will show you what is good.

**Read
Isaiah 1:10–20.**

Lord, lead me into the way of righteousness. I want to be about the Father's good business.

SEPTEMBER 29

Seek good, not evil, that you may live. Then the LORD God Almighty will be with you, just as you say he is.

—Amos 5:14 (NIV)

IT'S ALL GOOD

It seems like everything these days is made with a long list of ingredients. There are chemical additives for color, genetically improved ingredients for taste, and more additives for freshness, smell, and texture. Fortunately, I don't need a list of add-ons to make me who I am. All I need is goodness. And as long as you have me inside of you, you will always have goodness as well.

So when there are times that you think I'm telling you to stay away from something, chances are that something is actually bad for you. I hate evil, and the last thing God wants for you is something destructive in your life. I know that it can be hard sometimes to say no to things that don't seem all that bad, but that's why God gave you me. Think of me as your own evil detector. When I'm not saying, "It's all good," I can guarantee you that it's something to be avoided.

Read Amos 5:14–15.

Lord, help me to listen to you when I am tempted by evil things.

SEPTEMBER 30

*The LORD is good, a strong
refuge when trouble comes.
He is close to those who trust
in him.*

—**Nahum 1:7** (NLT)

A DRAWBRIDGE TO HOPE

Even Jesus didn't escape trouble. He, the Messiah and
Son of God, experienced hardship. But he knew what
to do when it came. In quietness with the Father, Jesus
found the refuge that Nahum wrote about. In prayer to
God, he found strength. In trusting the Lord's goodness,
he found peace.

Just as I was there for Jesus, I am there for you.
When hardships and troubles threaten to overwhelm you,
I am good. And the fruit of my goodness never rots or
goes bad. Others will disappoint. Your own strength can
fail. Mine does not. Trust in me, and I will be close to
you.

The fortress of my goodness is waiting. Cross over
the drawbridge and come inside. I can't wait to see you!

**Read
Nahum 1:7.** *You, Lord, are my refuge.
My hope is in you.*

OCTOBER

The Fruit of the Spirit: Faithfulness

OCTOBER 1

The fruit of the Spirit is . . . faithfulness.

—**Galatians 5:22** (ESV)

SAVOR THE FRUIT CALLED FAITHFULNESS

How I love the vows of faithfulness shared between husband and wife! Their words of commitment sparkle like precious gems on display.

Christ's faithfulness to the church, his beautiful bride, highlights this bond. He cares for and adores her in troubled times. He puts his bride first, loves the church without reservation—an aspect shown through his willingness to lay down his life to present her as perfect and spotless.

So it is with my fruit called faithfulness. When you push forward to a difficult goal—this is faithfulness. When you remember and keep whispered promises—this is faithfulness. When you stand firm for Jesus in the face of embarrassment, fear, and doubt—this is faithfulness.

I offer you my gift of enduring faithfulness, but you must choose it. I can help.

Read Galatians 5:16–26; 3 John 3.

Even in times of terrible trouble, Lord, teach me to be faithful to you.

OCTOBER 2

Your lovingkindness, O LORD,
extends to the heavens, Your
faithfulness reaches to the skies.

—**Psalm 36:5** (NASB)

YOU'RE NEVER ALONE

Beloved, the enemy employs many tricks in an attempt to separate you from me. One of the most common is to try to convince you that you are alone and unloved, that God has forgotten you.

Child, there is no limit to my love. You could never come close to exhausting it. There is nothing you could do and no place you could ever go where I will not be with you. I have promised to be with you always, and I keep all of my promises.

Hardships will come and there may be times when you feel lost and confused. In these times, remember that I know exactly where you are. You are too important for me to ever lose track of you. You are never alone; I am with you.

Read
Psalm 36:5–12.

Lord, I choose to stand on
the promise that you will
never abandon me.

OCTOBER 3

I will not withdraw My faithful love from him or betray My faithfulness.

—**Psalm 89:33** (HCSB)

WITH YOU ALWAYS

There are times when you do wrong, times when you disobey my Word and ignore my voice. In these times it may become necessary to chastise you. This may mean bringing discomfort or hardship into your life as a way of getting your attention and bringing you back to me. Just remember, in all of this, that I have not rejected you.

That will never happen. I will always love you. My faithfulness will follow you wherever you go. Not all hardships come as a result of discipline, but no matter the reason, I am by your side.

Even when you stray from me, I will never stray from you. I am with you always.

Read Psalm 89:19–37.

Thank you for your constant faithfulness to me, even when I don't deserve it.

OCTOBER 4

It is good to give thanks to the LORD and to sing praises to Your name, O Most High; to declare Your lovingkindness in the morning and Your faithfulness by night.

—Psalm 92:1–2 (NASB)

IT'S ALL GOOD

Whether your voice is on-key or off, your songs of praise are beautiful to me. Praise does not require the finest orchestra the world has to offer—just the music of your heart.

Child, I can help you have a heart of praise. Don't look at worship as an obligation or a task for which you have to dredge up feelings. I can help you see the beauty of praise by reminding you of the works of God. Consider the symphony of the oceans, the morning music of the birds, the harmony of the wind and the waving leaves. Let this music permeate your soul and build in you a song of praise, declaring my lovingkindness and faithfulness.

Read Psalm 92.

I praise you, O Lord Most High. I will give thanks to you in the morning and by night.

OCTOBER 5

The steadfast love of the LORD
never ceases;... great is your
faithfulness.

—**Lamentations 3:22–23**
(ESV)

GREAT FAITHFULNESS

The most enduring quality of the Father, the Son, and
I is faithfulness. The Father is faithful to everything
he has ever said, unwavering from the truth that defines
his trustworthiness. Jesus is faithful to complete the work
he has begun in your heart, and to forgive your every sin
when you repent. I am faithful to never leave you, to guide
you, to comfort you.

Every promise made in God's Word can be trusted.
Jesus demonstrated his faithfulness to his Father by dying
on a cross. The Father's compassion for you outweighed
the pain that his only Son endured, and it was all for you!

Likewise, remain steadfast in your faithfulness to
us. Listen to my leading, learn from the Bible, and pray
without ceasing. Great is the Lord's faithfulness; your
faithfulness in return will be greatly rewarded in glory.

Read
Lamentations
3:22–25.

Great is your faithfulness!
Help me to remain faithful,
Lord.

OCTOBER 6

God is faithful, by whom you were called into the fellowship of his Son, Jesus Christ our Lord.

—**1 Corinthians 1:9** (ESV)

GOD IS FAITHFUL

You are a child of God. The faithfulness of the Lord will carry you through your life.

Dear one, there is no need to fear the future—it is all planned out for you. There may be trials. There may be unfortunate consequences when you make poor decisions. There will be sadness. But rest assured, there also will be victories and blessings for good choices. I promise to wipe away every tear and bring joy everlasting.

Be skeptical of those who would try to separate us. Remain faithful to Jesus. This is not a burdensome task or unreasonable request. Trust and obey, and pray for those who attempt to come between us.

When the path seems uncertain, I am faithful to guide your every step. Lean on me. Listen to my voice. I will never lead you astray.

Read
1 Corinthians 1:4–9.

I trust your guidance, Lord, and will lean on you today.

OCTOBER 7

No temptation has overtaken you except what is common to mankind. And God is faithful; he will not let you be tempted beyond what you can bear.

—1 Corinthians 10:13 (NIV)

BURDENED FOR A PURPOSE

I know you believe sometimes that I have abandoned you. On the cross, Jesus experienced the reality of abandonment in a way that you will never have to experience. The Father had to turn his face from Jesus while Jesus assumed the burden of sin. Through Jesus' suffering, salvation was won. Now you can have a share in his victory.

When you endure trials and pain, I weep with you and intercede with groanings beyond words. In times of temptation, I am only a call for help away. Just as I led Jesus through his time of temptation, so I will lead you through any temptation.

No matter what circumstances you are bearing, you shall not be destroyed or overcome. I have tested you in order that you might become holy, the magnificent bride of Christ.

**Read
1 Corinthians
10:11–17.**

God, let me seek you out even during times of temptation. Remind me that you are my first love.

The one who calls you is faithful, and he will do it.

—1 Thessalonians 5:24 (NIV)

THE SPIRIT'S MISSION

Beloved, the victory is already won through Christ. Therefore I am pleased to dwell richly within God's children. Through the Son's death you are blameless in God's sight, and I will sustain you in righteousness forever. I am faithful to do it.

So go without fear! Rescue the lost and build one another up in love. Through my strength and the authority of Christ's name, you have been given everything you need. You are a coheir with Christ. The Alpha and Omega prepares the way before you. What fear or weakness can hold you back? Beloved, the powers of earth and hell cannot stop you any more than man can stop the seasons from changing or the wind from blowing.

Trust in my faithfulness. Charge forward, carrying my light into the darkness, confident in the knowledge that you have been found blameless before the Lord.

Read
1 Thessalonians
5:14–24.

God, remind me that you have already declared victory. Teach me to serve you faithfully.

OCTOBER 9

The Lord is faithful; he will strengthen you and guard you from the evil one.

—**2 Thessalonians 3:3** (NLT)

HE STRENGTHENS AND PROTECTS

Marriage, contracts, and pledges are all signs of commitment in a relationship. In our relationship, I am faithfully committed to you. You will have good days and bad days, thin days and fat days, but that will never affect my commitment to you. My faithfulness toward you is time tested and surpasses any circumstance. It is unbreakable.

In my faithfulness, I will be your protector in all the seasons of your life. Satan will attack you with anything he can find. He will use your fears, your insecurities, and your doubts. However, he cannot touch you unless he asks for the Father's permission. Even then, I will act as your Shield and Comforter.

Dear child, when you feel the attack of the enemy, ask me to help you. I will faithfully defend you in every season.

**Read
2 Thessalonians
3:1–5.**

Teach me to trust that you are faithful and will protect me, Lord.

OCTOBER 10

Christ was faithful as a Son over His house—whose house we are, if we hold fast our confidence and the boast of our hope firm until the end.

—**Hebrews 3:6** (NASB)

HOLD FAST

I am faithful, and I help God's children to be faithful as well. Faithfulness is not a characteristic that springs up overnight. It is shown through many years of making decisions and acting according to the principles in God's Word. Faithfulness is key, child.

If you are faithful to me, then you will listen to my voice and follow my direction as Jesus followed my lead. Sometimes it's hard for you to hear my voice over the volume of the world. When times are tough and you think I'm not listening, consider this: if you slow down and focus, you can hear me. Sometimes I may shout. Sometimes I may whisper. But either way, you must listen intentionally.

Listen closely and follow my lead. I will help you stay faithful.

Read Hebrews 3:1–6.

Loving Spirit, help me to remain faithful.

So then, those who suffer according to God's will should commit themselves to their faithful Creator and continue to do good.

—1 Peter 4:19 (NIV)

COMMITMENT TO THE CREATOR

As much as I wanted to, I could not promise my servants an easy life. Indeed, they would soon face greater hardship than anyone had faced before. For my name's sake, they were insulted, beaten, tortured, and even executed. It hurt my heart to watch them suffer so much, but I was proud of them. They knew and trusted me and displayed steadfast commitment to righteousness through times of trial and peace.

Beloved, I cannot guarantee a life of ease for you either. The world is not always a pleasant place, even for those who are of it. Heartache, rejection, and disappointment are common experiences, and because you bear my name, you may even suffer persecution.

But you can take comfort because I have conquered the world, loved one. In the midst of sufferings great and small, never tire of doing good. Your faithful Creator is with you always.

**Read
1 Peter 4:12–19.**

Lord God, let me live a life that is faithfully committed to you.

OCTOBER 12

The Lord has shown unfailing love and faithfulness to my master, for he has led me straight to my master's relatives.

—**Genesis 24:27** (NLT)

UNFAILING LOVE AND FAITHFULNESS

When Abraham sent his servant to find a wife for Isaac, he didn't worry about the outcome. He was convinced that a woman for his son to marry would be found at the right time and in the right place. You see, Abraham had become a man of faith after witnessing the faithfulness of God over and over again. He knew the love of God never fails.

What a delight it is for me when children of faith journey through life with a trusting spirit instead of a fearful heart. The very thing for which you are seeking guidance is of concern to me. Be it a future mate, a new job, a place to live, or a congregation with whom to worship, I will guide you. You can be sure of that!

Read Genesis 24:1–27.

Give me eyes to see your faithfulness. May my faith be fed by what I see.

OCTOBER 13

Swear to me by the LORD,
since I have shown you
kindness, that you also will
show kindness to my father's
house.

—Joshua 2:12 (NKJV)

OPEN TO OBEY

Rahab's reputation left much to be desired. But her future was not defined by her past. Though she had seduced men with her beauty, I wooed her with grace. Rahab's willingness to help the two spies indicated an openness to obey God. Every day you have that same opportunity.

It is my nature to draw those with willing hearts to the Father's heart. No act of disobedience from yesterday disqualifies you from what you were designed to do today. Beloved, don't let the shame of past defeats prevent you from knowing the victory of obedience. I am with you to strengthen you. I will whisper reminders of God's faithfulness to you. Even as Rahab's desire to do the right thing resulted in her entire family's safety, your cooperation with the Father's desires will influence your family toward goodness. Don't doubt my ability to wipe your slate clean. Trust me.

Read
Joshua 2:12–15.

Forgetting the past and all of its disappointments, I give myself anew today, Lord.

OCTOBER 14

Solomon said, "You have shown great and steadfast love to your servant David my father, because he walked before you in faithfulness, in righteousness."

—1 Kings 3:6 (ESV)

HIS FAITHFULNESS NEVER CEASES

People are far from perfect, but as the Spirit of truth, I recognize hearts that strive to honor the Lord despite failings and mistakes. Like David, even the greatest of sinners can find mercy and grace, for God respects honest repentance. When a heart is contrite, a will is subdued, and a soul is regretful of mistakes, truth can be restored and holy fellowship can be reestablished.

The desire of every believer should be to follow the mandates of the Lord in strict obedience. When sins are committed, I hear your prayers of contrition, and bonds of love are formed anew.

Follow me. Walk in faithfulness and in righteousness, and I will be with you every step of the way.

Read
1 Kings 3:4–14.

Help me walk before you in faithfulness and righteousness, Lord, and keep me united with you.

OCTOBER 15

I have not hidden Your righteousness within my heart; I have spoken of Your faithfulness and Your salvation.

—**Psalm 40:10** (NASB)

PROCLAIMING GOD'S FAITHFULNESS

It is natural to proclaim the joys of your heart. Will the young woman fail to tell all her friends of her engagement? Will the hunter or fisherman not regale his comrades with stories of his quests? Will the parent not brag about the son or daughter who excels? It is in your nature to broadcast your joyous news to others.

What then can be the limits of proclaiming the wonders of God's power, his awesomeness, his wisdom, his provision, his glory! Do I, the Spirit of gratitude, not reveal to everyone the majestic glory of God? Is God's goodness and faithfulness not so marvelous that each tongue is inspired to be a clarion call of praise to the Almighty?

Read Psalm 40.

Lord, I embrace the strength you give me to proclaim your wondrous glory.

OCTOBER 16

*Your faithful love is as high as
the heavens; Your faithfulness
reaches the clouds.*

—**Psalm 57:10** (HCSB)

TRUST ME

I could describe the heavens to you, but there are no
words in the human tongue to define such greatness. It
is unfathomable, as is the Father's faithfulness. Humanity
struggles to understand it, because it is incomprehensible.
This is where you must have faith.

Even when your world is crashing down, you must
trust that the Father will come through for you. Circumstances may not be what you desire, but he promises joy
that is eternal, not momentary. He plans for your good
and will never leave you nor forsake you.

I will always remain faithful. I will never lead you
astray or down a path too great for you to handle. The
Father sent me to help, guide, and interpret for you. Trust
me. Trust the immeasurable reach of the Father's faithful
love.

**Read
Psalm 57.**

*Thank you for having
faithfulness too great for
me to understand.*

OCTOBER 17

I will also praise you with the harp for your faithfulness, O my God; I will sing praises to you with the lyre, O Holy One of Israel.

—**Psalm 71:22** (ESV)

FAITHFUL PRAISE

Will you sing for me? I raised you up and brought you to redemption. I am filled with joy regarding you. Will you praise me?

David praised me with the harp, the lyre, and with shouts. I have given you love, and I rejoice when you acknowledge my presence and love me in return. In whatever way your praise comes to me, its beauty always pleases me.

You prove your faith by trusting me and being grateful for what I have done for you. When you praise me for my gifts, I glory in your verbal offering.

I want to share in everything that is good with you. Do not forget all the things that I have done in my love for you.

Read Psalm 71. *I praise you for your blessings. Help me to grow closer to you through my praise.*

Let love and faithfulness never leave you; bind them around your neck, write them on the tablet of your heart.

—**Proverbs 3:3** (NIV)

SECRET TO A GOOD NAME

Child, I hear people talk of the secret to a good name and winning favor with others. Some have said a good reputation is based on popularity that comes from success, fame, or financial achievement. Others say a good reputation is built upon a history of good deeds and kind words. But if your credibility is built upon a foundation of circumstances and not upon a foundation of the heart, then all will begin to crumble the instant difficulties and trials arise.

Beloved, my desire is that you will store in your heart my deep and abiding love for you; that you will allow me to fill you with faithfulness. Then, as you go forth into your day, no matter what circumstances you encounter, you will never let my love and faithfulness leave you. You will always find the right way to respond. Life will not distract or derail you. Then you will have my favor and a good reputation with others.

Read
Proverbs 3:1–4.

Spirit, write upon my heart your love and faithfulness. Never let me forget them.

If you plan to do evil, you will be lost; if you plan to do good, you will receive unfailing love and faithfulness.

—**Proverbs 14:22** (NLT)

REAP WHAT YOU SOW

No one who plants a garden with tomato seeds would expect a crop of cucumbers. What you plant, you will surely gather when the crop grows. This is a law of nature. So it should not come as a surprise that this truth applies spiritually. If you indulge in gossip about your friends with others, don't be surprised when you lose those friendships. If you lie to your boss about your abilities, don't be surprised when you are passed over for a promotion.

Child, every action has a result. If you invest your time in pursuing worldly goals and not godly ones, you will be lost. But if you sow good works and pursue the things that please me, then you will most surely reap the benefits of my unfailing love and faithfulness. What do you intend to plant today?

Read Proverbs 14:22–35.

Dear Lord, help me to plant good things today and grant me your unfailing love and faithfulness.

OCTOBER 20

For the dead cannot praise you; they cannot raise their voices in praise. . . . Only the living can praise you as I do today. Each generation tells of your faithfulness to the next.

—Isaiah 38:18–19 (NLT)

THE FAITHFULNESS OF GOD

The Lord is faithful and will not abandon those who seek him. When Hezekiah, king of Judah, learned that he was about to die, he prayed. He thought he had to argue his way into healing. All he had to do was cry for help. According to his sovereign will, the Father healed Hezekiah. Hezekiah responded in praise, his faith in the Lord strengthened.

Likewise, dear one, your cries for help will never go unanswered. They may not be answered exactly as you intend, but I will always respond with compassion.

I know your situation at all times—your fears and your doubts. You never have to convince me to be faithful; I cannot be otherwise. Let the truth of my faithfulness strengthen your faith and inspire you to praise.

Read
Isaiah 38:9–20.

Praise you, Lord, for your faithfulness and compassion.

OCTOBER 21

And I will betroth you to Me in faithfulness. Then you will know the LORD.

—**Hosea 2:20** (NASB)

REFRESHMENT IN THE CLEARING

There's a gentle wind softly whistling through the trees right now. Just ahead there's a clearing where we can talk. Come back to me today. It's been a long time. You went after other people and things that you thought would make you happy. You gave to them what I provided for you. You forgot me and wandered far from me.

Yet I didn't forget you. And now is the time for restoration. I want to give you back the vineyards that were destroyed, the coverings that were taken, and put the praise of my name back on your tongue. The wind is still gentle. The clearing in the wilderness is waiting. You don't need to run from me. My face is turned toward you. My hands are outstretched. My voice is kind. Come, join me there. Renew and refresh yourself with my faithfulness. And then you will know me once again.

Read Hosea 2:14–23.

Lord, I'm in need of renewal. I am grateful for your faithfulness.

He has shown you, O man, what is good; and what does the LORD require of you but to do justly, to love mercy, and to walk humbly with your God?

—**Micah 6:8** (NKJV)

WALK THIS WAY

Do you think I require a grand gesture of obedience on your part?

Stop believing the lie that a worldwide ministry, a dazzling display of disciples, or a best-selling book is the template of an effective walk with Jesus. Child, every life is precious to me—every walk with Jesus is different and valued. You were not created to be a carbon copy of someone else. You were made to follow my leading in a way that is tailored especially for you.

I require faithfulness. Faithfulness starts in the heart. Being faithful in the little things grows into a lifestyle of obedience. I will always guide you in what's good.

Read
Micah 6:6–8.

Lord, let my love for you become faithfulness, and help me to live faithfully in every aspect of my life.

OCTOBER 23

*What if some were
unfaithful? Will their
unfaithfulness nullify God's
faithfulness? Not at all!*

—**Romans 3:3–4** (NIV)

ALWAYS FAITHFUL

D ear one, though you sometimes struggle in your
beliefs, I do not change. I have always been faithful,
and I will always be faithful. There is nothing that can
change that, not even unbelief. In the midst of a world
where you are bombarded with doubt, remember that I am
constant and a God of integrity.

When you feel as though the people around you are
full of lies and deceit, remember that I am true. Look to
me for truth. I will never lie to you or lead you astray.
The world will try to pull you away in every direction, but
rely on God's inerrant Word. You will be justified on the
day you stand before him.

You will face much until that day. Call on me. I will
be true, even as you wander. I will wait for you, faithfully,
to call on me.

**Read
Romans 3:1–8.**

*Divine Spirit, thank you
for remaining faithful and
true, even in my wandering.*

OCTOBER 24

*[Demonstrate] utter faithfulness,
so that they may adorn the
teaching of God our Savior in
everything.*

—**Titus 2:10** (HCSB)

NEW BEGINNINGS

Before Jesus came into your life, you were a slave to sin. It affected every part of you. No matter how hard you tried to be free from it, sin was the master of your life. Then Jesus entered in and broke the shackles of sin. In their place, he gave you a new beginning and his promise to never leave you. Now let me help you be faithful in return.

Faithfulness is a characteristic of obedience to Jesus. This was Paul's charge to Titus. Faithfulness keeps a worker on task even though a boss is cruel. It helps a friend speak with kindness about another friend who has betrayed him.

Take heart, for I am with you. The Father sent me to help you discern his will. When you faithfully follow my lead, others will see and desire to meet your Savior.

**Read
Titus 2:6–14.**

*Lord, may I be faithful to
you even when everyone
else says otherwise. Help
me follow your lead.*

OCTOBER 25

Dear friend, you are being faithful to God when you care for the traveling teachers who pass through, even though they are strangers to you.

—3 John 5 (NLT)

A SUPPORTIVE FAMILY

You are part of an extraordinary family. When you became united with Christ, you joined a family with a Father who loves you dearly and has blessed you greatly. In him, you gained brothers and sisters. The Father put them in your life to help support you, care for you, and show you his love.

And just as they are here to support you, you are also here to be a blessing to them. Beloved, when you see that one of your brothers or sisters has a need—fill it, just as John commended Gaius.

When you choose to show the Father's love to his children through your actions, the Father sees your faithfulness to the gospel. Let God's love and faithfulness flow out of you today.

Read
3 John.

Please help me be faithful to you by supporting the needs of my brothers and sisters in Christ.

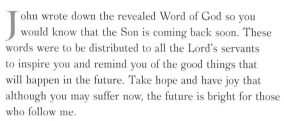

OCTOBER 26

The angel said to me, "These words are trustworthy and true. The Lord, the God who inspires the prophets, sent his angel to show his servants the things that must soon take place."

—**Revelation 22:6** (NIV)

COMING SOON

John wrote down the revealed Word of God so you would know that the Son is coming back soon. These words were to be distributed to all the Lord's servants to inspire you and remind you of the good things that will happen in the future. Take hope and have joy that although you may suffer now, the future is bright for those who follow me.

Just like John, you too must spread the word of the Son's return. Tell your family, friends, and yes, even your enemies. Once you were like them, a sinful creature wrapped up in yourself. Now that you have accepted Jesus, you've become a child of God. Your reward awaits.

Be ready for the Son's grand return. Make sure that you are following God's ways and thus able to give an account of your actions. Share the words I have given you.

Read Revelation 22:6–9.

Help me, Lord, to live every day on earth as though it could be my last.

OCTOBER 27

I saw heaven opened, and a white horse was standing there. Its rider was named Faithful and True, for he judges fairly and wages a righteous war.

—**Revelation 19:11** (NLT)

THE RIDER IS FAITHFUL

The Son of God's banner is the gospel—the good news that by one man's sacrifice, all have the opportunity to know truth. All have the opportunity to choose.

Each person on this planet will declare allegiance to Jesus or reject him altogether. Who will you serve? The king and commander called Christ? Or the lowly ruler of this decaying world?

The man upon a white horse leads the charge against unrighteousness. Rejoice! He holds the reigns of truth tightly and he will defend you, his child, against accusations of sin and unfaithfulness. Even those who now hold God's Son in disdain will one day bow before him in worship and respect.

Read
Revelation
19:11–16.

Father, I rejoice and give thanks for the faithfulness of Jesus.

OCTOBER 28

Do not fear any of those things which you are about to suffer.... Be faithful until death, and I will give you the crown of life.

—Revelation 2:10 (NKJV)

FAITHFULNESS, NOT FEAR

I know the idea of testing sounds uncomfortable to you. Yet you have been promised power through my fruit of love and self-control. Turn timidity aside, beloved. Believers in Christ have access to my power in abundance.

You can always pray, child. God alone deserves your trust, but not just on days when the sun shines and you have money in your pocket. Even when shadows loom, I want you to believe that he is good.

I cannot promise that you will be free from trials or temptations. In your life here on earth, they are guaranteed. But I am with you to help you and love you till the end. Someday you will wear the crown of life, if you stand firm and faithful. Listen! Christ is calling to you with words of hope and life.

Read Revelation 2:8–11.

I know that Jesus triumphs. Keep me faithful until the end.

OCTOBER 29

If we confess our sins, he is faithful and just and will forgive us our sins and purify us from all unrighteousness.

—1 John 1:9 (NIV)

HE IS FAITHFUL

Consider this, precious one: every time you do wrong and ask me to forgive you, I will forgive you and cleanse you. Every time. I am faithful to forgive.

Because of Jesus, you can be cleansed and forgiven. Your sins will no longer be a broken bridge between us. The cross of Jesus erased those sins—those and any sin you will ever commit—effectively bridging the chasm between us. This is not a license to sin, merely an invitation to be healed and cleansed.

You no longer have to carry the burden of sin. Just talk to me. I will listen to you and cleanse you.

Read
1 John 1:5–9.

Days go by, and thunder claps, yet I'm still reminded of your faithfulness in the storms.

OCTOBER 30

The Lord is slow to anger,
abounding in love and forgiving
sin and rebellion. Yet he does
not leave the guilty unpunished.
—**Numbers 14:18** (NIV)

FAITHFUL AND JUST

I am neither easily frustrated nor easily angered. Because I am love, I pour out love for the children of God. I forgive because I am merciful and gracious. Though you sin, I am always willing to forgive you with an open heart.

I not only am a loving God, I am also a just and good Judge. A good judge punishes the guilty. As I told my servants Moses and Aaron, I will punish the guilty and the children of the guilty from generation to generation because they follow their parents' footsteps instead of following my ways.

You, however, don't have to face my wrath, child. Faith in Jesus exempts you from that. In the death of Jesus the justice that my righteous anger demanded was achieved.

Read
Numbers 14:10–18.

Find comfort in God's love, and remember it is only by His love and grace you are saved.

He keeps the feet of His godly ones, but the wicked ones are silenced in darkness; for not by might shall a man prevail.

—1 Samuel 2:9 (NASB)

PROCLAIMING FAITHFULNESS

Hannah kept her word. As she did, I kept watch over her feet on the path. And after she weaned her son—the son I gave her—Hannah brought him to me as she said she would. Then she prayed a beautiful song of praise and thanksgiving. She told of her salvation and proclaimed my holiness, knowledge, and power.

Dear one, depend on me as Hannah did. There are some situations that require my strength and faithfulness, not the efforts of man. I guard the steps of the faithful. Pick my fruit of faithfulness today and let it nourish and undergird you on the journey. And when others don't understand your faithfulness to me, I see it. And I will reward it.

Read
1 Samuel 1:19—
2:11.

Lord, thank you for your faithfulness. Help me walk in faithfulness with you.

NOVEMBER
The Fruit of the Spirit: Gentleness

NOVEMBER 1

The Holy Spirit produces this kind of fruit in our lives: . . . gentleness.

—**Galatians 5:22–23** (NLT)

SAVOR THE FRUIT CALLED GENTLENESS

My gift of gentleness should never be mistaken for weak resolve. Great strength is required to kneel before someone smaller. Inwardly you may wish to push ahead, but your gentleness allows others to take the favored position instead.

Some would rather rely on violence and force. Those who embrace gentleness put up with mockery from those who don't understand it.

My spiritual gift of gentleness is inherently good. It allows a husky man to hug his aging mother. It permits a tired mom to nurse a sobbing newborn. It involves soft hands washing a body racked with disease. Gentleness is the way you respond in Jesus' love to those who crave encouragement. It is the quiet voice that touches a chord deep within and offers hope when it is needed most.

Read
Galatians 5:16–26;
Philippians 4:5.

Spirit of the Living God, help me respond to others with your gentleness and to open hard hearts by my example.

NOVEMBER 2

Now I, Paul, myself am pleading with you by the meekness and gentleness of Christ—who in presence am lowly among you, but being absent am bold toward you.

—**2 Corinthians 10:1** (NKJV)

ONE QUIET POWER

The world celebrates the squeaky wheel, the one with the loudest voice demanding to be heard. Child, I celebrate the meekness and gentleness of the Savior. Gentleness is powerful.

Jesus knew when to use righteous anger, but in many of his dealings with others, his gentleness and compassion stirred the heart. The One who could have commanded a legion of angels to do his bidding chose to walk humbly. He acted gently toward sinners who asked for forgiveness. He acted gently toward his persecutors. What strength there is in meekness!

Paul's gentle exhortation still impacts the heart centuries later. Appeal to others with gentleness. With my help, your gentle actions can be more powerful than an army.

Read
2 Corinthians
10:1–6.

Dear Father, help me to act with gentleness toward others. Pattern my words after the words of your Son.

NOVEMBER 3

With all humility and gentleness, with patience, [show] tolerance for one another in love.

—**Ephesians 4:2** (NASB)

WITH GENTLENESS

What is it that sets the people of God apart from every false religion or movement of the day? It is the fact that I can change people's hearts and bind them together in Christ. I do not merely change the outward behavior. I supply true humility, gentleness, and patience, helping them show tolerance and love for one another. In this I also unify all believers.

Every sin, every weakness, can be forgiven and turned into a blessing for the kingdom. Therefore be gentle with one another; love as I have loved you.

When you deal with others gently, when you speak calmly, when you react carefully, and when you humbly understand others' shortcomings (since you have your own), then you are building the kingdom—one gentle act and word at a time.

Read
Ephesians 4:1–7.

Lord, help me to shine your light to the world. Guide my steps to those who need you most.

*Let your gentle spirit be known
to all men. The Lord is near.*

—**Philippians 4:5** (NASB)

MAKE HIS GENTLENESS KNOWN

I alone can give you satisfaction in all things. The things of this world can grant temporary happiness. They cannot give you the true joy that is found only in me.

Because you have me, you don't need to strive and fight for the things this world has to offer. Instead, be gentle. Let my peace show through you so that the world may take notice.

Even in difficult times, I am always with you. Rejoice in your suffering, and through it learn the truths I am teaching you. You are my representative among the lost, dear one, and I want you to be my hands and feet. Demonstrate my love with joy, and minister with a gentle spirit to those who need the peace I offer.

**Read
Philippians 4:4–9.**

*God, give me the
gentleness to demonstrate
your peace to the lost and
the seeking.*

NOVEMBER 5

So, as those who have been chosen of God, holy and beloved, put on a heart of compassion, kindness, humility, gentleness and patience.

—**Colossians 3:12** (NASB)

BEAUTY IN GENTLENESS

The quiet presence and gentle words of a loving friend can encourage in times of discomfort. A gentle word quiets those who are hurting and soothes those who are ill at ease. So too, the opportunity to be the comforter when someone else is feeling low is good for the soul. Such an exchange can be a blessing to both people, for gentleness and compassion are inspiring qualities.

I love to witness these moments. It is beautiful to see you together, living out the love you have been shown.

Do not be afraid to come alongside someone in need and offer that person the comfort of a gentle hand. Let me guide you, giving you the appropriate words and the appropriate silence.

Read
Colossians 3:12–17.

Lord, help me put on a heart of gentleness and use me to be an encouragement to someone, that you may be glorified.

NOVEMBER 6

*Be peaceable and considerate,
and always ... be gentle toward
everyone.*

—Titus 3:2 (NIV)

COMPASSION FOR THE LOST

In every circumstance, show gentleness toward everyone. This is what you have been called to do as a follower of Christ. Though he was mocked, persecuted, beaten, and scorned by his own people, Jesus responded with gentleness because his compassion for his oppressors surpassed their contempt for him.

He had compassion because he knew how lost they were. And so were you once. But you were rescued through Christ's sacrifice.

For this reason, I want you to be a living example of light to those around you. Let me ignite your compassion when you look on those who are lost and searching. I will fill you with the fruit of gentleness that comes from me.

Read
Titus 3:1–11.

*Let the knowledge of
my redemption fill me
with compassion and
gentleness today.*

NOVEMBER 7

Always being prepared to make a defense to anyone who asks you for a reason for the hope that is in you; yet do it with gentleness and respect.

—1 Peter 3:15 (ESV)

YOUR DEFENSE

Over the centuries I've viewed the tall, round towers of the Celtic monks and the fortified strongholds of Norman kings. Their stone ramparts commanded respect. Every weak spot in the stronghold was guarded well and every strong point armed to the teeth.

When you defend your faith, it's good for you to be prepared, to "arm yourself," as it were. Study the Word and practice telling your story. You may not be able to anticipate every question or concern, but you can be well prepared with what *you* know. And when you share your faith, always be gentle and respectful. Don't look down on others or act in a prideful manner. Remember where you came from; remember what we have done in your life. Then, with preparation, gentleness, and respect, fearlessly tell others about us.

A dying world needs to know the good news.

Read
1 Peter 3:8–17.

Lord, give me respectful defenses so that my faith might be regarded as a cherished love.

NOVEMBER 8

*The Lord's servant must not
be quarrelsome but kind to
everyone, able to teach, patiently
enduring evil, correcting his
opponents with gentleness.*

—2 Timothy 2:24–25 (ESV)

I AM GENTLE

Just as I instruct you, so you must instruct others. Just as I am forgiving of you, so you must be forgiving of others. I am prepared to use you as an instrument by which to spread my glory, but you must seek to follow me in gentleness and in humility.

My truth is not arrogant. The Son was gentle with his disciples and served them. In this way, he left an example for them to follow. Child, you can follow that example by showing respect for others.

Approach error softly so that it may be removed and many people saved. Truth is not a hammer with which to hit someone. It grows slowly in the heart of the lost and can release those in bondage.

Read
2 Timothy 2:22–26.

*Please help me to see
myself as a gentle servant
to others.*

NOVEMBER 9

You, Timothy, are a man of God; so run from all these evil things. Pursue righteousness and . . . gentleness.

—1 Timothy 6:11 (NLT)

GRASP FOR GENTLENESS

The love of money is fueled by passion. But it is the wrong kind of passion. It is fueled by self-passion. So not only is it the opposite of my fruit, gentleness, but also, as Paul wrote, "the love of money is the root of all kinds of evil" (1 Timothy 6:10 NLT). I encourage you, as Paul encouraged Timothy, to pursue gentleness.

Strive to be like Christ because you are his witness on earth. Remembering that he was gentle and compassionate, strive toward gentleness. You are in a battle with a world that wants you to be aggressive. It wants you to grasp for worldly things. Run from evil passions, and pursue gentleness.

Read
1 Timothy 6:9–14.

Strengthen my resolve, Lord, to be gentle. I yield my will to you.

NOVEMBER 10

The wisdom from above is first pure, then peaceable, gentle, open to reason, full of mercy and good fruits, impartial and sincere.

—James 3:17 (ESV)

GENTLE WISDOM

When Jesus came into the world, he did not condemn sinners. He walked, talked, and ate with them. The Son spoke wisdom and treated the estranged with gentleness. When false accusers nailed him to the cross, he asked the Father to forgive them.

This is why his ministry was fruitful. People wanted to be with him because they knew he would change their lives. He was patient with their misunderstandings and accepting of their faults. Follow the Son's way, for it is the path of wisdom.

When you call for the Father's understanding, remember that I will not guide you toward a manner of darkness. In all your ways, seek the Father so you can understand my promptings and be discerning in the choices you make. Approach others lovingly, and pursue the wisdom of gentleness.

Read
James 3:17–18.

Help me to hear and understand your wisdom, so I can love others with gentleness.

NOVEMBER 11

A gentle answer deflects anger, but harsh words make tempers flare.

—**Proverbs 15:1** (NLT)

THE POWER OF GENTLENESS

D ear one, how powerful is the tongue you have been given! You must govern it carefully. The difference between truth and deceit, peace and rivalry, love and selfishness, rests within your words. I gave you the gift of speech so that you could encourage rather than damage, promote wisdom rather than idleness, and praise rather than curse. I am here to help you bear this responsibility.

When someone slanders your name or speaks harshly to you, listen to me and do not strike back. Returning wrath for wrath is like fighting fire with fire. Destruction is all that can result. Instead, I will give you a gentle answer to their spiteful words and wisdom for their foolishness. Like cool water thrown upon a flame, your gentleness will put out their anger.

Overcome burning words of hatred with healing gentleness. Look to me for guidance in your words today.

Read
Proverbs 15:1–7.

Gracious Father, please help me to use my mouth responsibly. Let me respond to harshness with gentleness.

NOVEMBER 12

Through patience a ruler can be persuaded, and a gentle tongue can break a bone.

—**Proverbs 25:15** (NIV)

PATIENCE AND GENTLENESS

Patience is a powerful thing. It allows you to see others through discerning eyes. It helps you to understand the best way to cope with difficult circumstances. In being patient, you give the world a glimpse of who I am.

Patience and gentleness go together. You cannot be patient and harsh at the same time, or gentle and impatient. They do not mix well. But I am rich in both patience and gentleness, so when you struggle with either one, you can look to me. I will give you the grace you need.

Patience isn't easy, but I will provide it. Patience does not come naturally to you. But as you grow in me, you will grow in patience, and gentleness will follow. Of this you can be sure.

Read
Proverbs 25:11–17.

Spirit of grace, help me to grow in patience and gentleness so I can honor you.

NOVEMBER 13

*Take my yoke upon you,
and learn from me, for I
am gentle and lowly in heart,
and you will find rest for
your souls.*

—Matthew 11:29 (ESV)

CLOTHED IN GENTLENESS

Jesus came to earth in complete humility. His first bed was a feedbox for animals. This would be a model for his life and ministry. From teaching children to eating meals with tax collectors to dying a criminal's death on a cross, the Savior was truly gentle and humble in all he did. As a child of God, I want you also to be gentle and humble.

The world you live in makes it difficult to be gentle or humble. After all, it is in your very nature to pridefully look out for yourself. But, dear child, pride puts a wedge between you and the Father. Come to me and find freedom from this burden. I will clothe you in humility and gentleness so others may see Christ at work in you.

Each time you place another's interests before your own, you follow Christ's example and allow me to work through you. In this way, the Father is pleased.

Read
Matthew 11:25–30.

Father, I seek forgiveness for my pride. Today, please help me follow Jesus' example of humility and gentleness.

NOVEMBER 14

The gentle are blessed, for they will inherit the earth.

—**Matthew 5:5** (HCSB)

A DISPOSITION OF GENTLENESS

Beloved, I see you falter in your walk with Jesus when others hurt you or treat you with contempt. You wonder if might really does make right or if gentleness is really foolishness.

Don't adhere to the ways of the world or its vain philosophies. The world would have you believe that gentleness makes you weak and strips you of respect. But I resist the arrogant and steadfastly overturn the plans of those who set their faces against me. Though they seem to prosper now, the Day of Judgment is coming.

Be encouraged! Believe the words of the Son. Those who are gentle will inherit the earth.

Read
Matthew 5:1–12.

Father, may your will be done in my life. I want to be gentle in spirit as I follow after you.

NOVEMBER 15

Brothers, if someone is caught in any wrongdoing, you who are spiritual should restore such a person with a gentle spirit.

—**Galatians 6:1** (HCSB)

GENTLE RESTORATION

Beloved, as a member of the body of Christ, you have the privilege of giving and receiving the support of others.

There will come a time when someone will be wooed by sin, and you may have to confront that person. When you are the one approaching your brother or sister in Christ, do not have a judgmental attitude or boast about your strength against sin. Instead, speak gently and humbly. Lead the person back to the righteous path for his or her own good and not for your egotistical desire. Be careful when helping, for it is easy for your sinful nature to make you proud.

Ask me for just the right words to say. I will help you and give you wisdom so you will be a guide to those who stray.

Read Galatians 6:1–5.

Lord, guard my tongue as I gently confront those who have gone astray.

NOVEMBER 16

*Although we could have been
a burden as Christ's apostles,
instead we were gentle among
you, as a nursing mother
nurtures her own children.*

—1 Thessalonians 2:7 (HCSB)

GENTLE SPIRIT

The apostle Paul was an authority figure in the lives of the early Christians. But his authority was not marked by a dictatorial style. He chose the metaphor of a mother to describe his position of leadership in their lives. I prompted him to do that.

Consider the words used in Scripture to describe my presence in your world: *comforter, advocate, helper.* They are gentle words because I am gentle. Think of a young mother embracing her newborn. That intimate embrace is a picture of my quiet companionship with you. When you draw near to me, I will draw near to you and gently nourish you with the milk of truth. And while I may at times discipline you, as does a mother who loves her child, even then I will do so gently.

I love you.

Read
1 Thessalonians
2:7–8.

*Lord, I cherish your
gentle way with me and
long to be drawn closer.*

NOVEMBER 17

Now the overseer is to be above reproach ... respectable, hospitable, able to teach, not given to drunkenness, not violent but gentle.

—1 Timothy 3:2–3 (NIV)

LEADERS ARE GENTLE

What should leaders of Christ's body look like? That's a question the apostle Paul attempted to answer as local congregations were planted. When he outlined the qualifications for leadership within the local church, he was not simply addressing the needs and challenges of his culture; he was not basing his list on his own ideas. I communicated those qualities to him. Those qualities—gentleness, patience, and respect—reflect the heart of the Trinity.

What is expected of human leaders in the church is what we, the Godhead, make possible. Let that encourage you as you submit to the leaders in your local fellowship or assume a leadership position. And to the degree that you have been wounded by Christian leaders who have not led in the way Paul described, allow me to heal your bruised emotions.

Read
1 Timothy 3:2–4.

Lord, I'm grateful to know that gentleness is a quality that originates in heaven.

NOVEMBER 18

Your beauty . . . should consist of what is inside the heart with the imperishable quality of a gentle and quiet spirit, which is very valuable in God's eyes.

—1 Peter 3:3–4 (HCSB)

TRUE BEAUTY

Child, it's so easy to be deluded into thinking that beauty comes from the outside. One only has to follow what's popular in magazines, on television, or on the Internet to know that the world values those who are physically beautiful. It celebrates those who wear beautiful clothes, have elaborate hairstyles, and adorn themselves with the finest jewelry. But styles change, beauty fades, and what is valued in one season is discarded in the next.

True beauty that lasts and that is prized above all is that which comes from the heart. I cherish a gentle and quiet spirit that springs forth from my presence in you. Those qualities will never change, fade, or go out of style. They will always be beautiful to me.

That is how holy people through the ages made themselves beautiful. It's how you can be beautiful today.

Read 1 Peter 3:1–6.

Holy Spirit, fill me with your gentleness and quiet spirit, so that my true beauty will shine through.

NOVEMBER 19

He trains my hands for war,
so that my arms can bend
a bow of bronze. You have
given me the shield of your
salvation, and your gentleness
made me great.

—**2 Samuel 22:35–36** (ESV)

THE WAY TO GREATNESS

From the time David stood against the giant Goliath to his victories over Israel's bitter enemies to eluding the murderous intent of King Saul, he relied on the God of Israel. David acknowledged my help in preparing him for battle, for being his strong fortress, his shield, his strength. Yet even as he offered his praises for victory over his enemies, David also said, "Your gentleness made me great."

Gentleness on the battlefield? A gentle warrior? Yes, child, there is strength in a gentle spirit. It can do as much to subdue an enemy as strength. When David caught King Saul in the cave, he didn't overpower Saul by a show of force. No, Saul was moved by David's gentleness and compassion toward him.

In the battles you face today, ask for my fruit of gentleness. It is the way to true greatness.

Read
2 Samuel 22.

Empower me today, Lord,
with your strength and
your gentleness. Help me to
treat even my enemies with
compassion.

NOVEMBER 20

You have also given me the shield of Your salvation; Your right hand has held me up, Your gentleness has made me great.

—**Psalm 18:35** (NKJV)

STILL AT WAR

We are at war. When the Son died on the cross for your sins, a spiritual battle was won. Satan's plans fell apart. The war did not end there, though. Satan is not yet defeated. In the end, the Son will triumph over the evil one with all my glory. Until then you will be accosted with the temptations of this world. You will lose if you try to defeat them with your own strength.

I will act as a shield for you, blocking the flaming arrows of the evil one. I will train you, not allowing you to have more than you can withstand. You can lean on me when you are weary of this battle. I will hold you up. With my gentleness, I will make you great.

When you come up against adversity and temptation, you will triumph with me by your side. Ask me to accompany you into battle before you get out of bed. Speak with me and let me guide your movements to safety.

Read
Psalm 18:30–36.

Holy Spirit, give me the strength to stand strong against the evil one and not give in to his temptations.

A gentle tongue is a tree of life, but perverseness in it breaks the spirit.

—**Proverbs 15:4** (ESV)

A GENTLE TONGUE

Words hold power to hurt or to heal. Imagine two trees sitting on top of a hill. One tree is bursting with life, its strong branches effortlessly holding green leaves and nestling wild creatures. The other tree sits with drooping, broken branches, its bark withered and riddled with jagged holes. This is how I see the effects of your words. When you build up and encourage others with gentle words, their spirits blossom like the first tree. If your words are spiteful and cutting, you are hurting another one of God's children. What is the intention of your words? You choose what effect you will have on the people around you.

Beloved, you understand these hurts from experience. Think carefully about what you say, and ask me to help you with your words. A tree's roots are always reaching toward life in the form of water. Just as roots seek water, seek my gentle words.

Read
Proverbs 15:1–4.

Today, Father, guide my words to heal, not hurt.

NOVEMBER 22

But I was like a docile lamb brought to the slaughter; and I did not know that they had devised schemes against me.

—**Jeremiah 11:19** (NKJV)

BE GENTLE AND STILL

I know that you sometimes feel completely alone. The trust you place in others crumbles, leaving a hole of doubt in relationships you once considered strong. You have even wondered why you are being singled out and ostracized.

The prophet Jeremiah experienced those same feelings when he learned his enemies were trying to kill him for proclaiming the Lord's name. But the Lord punished the plotters and defended his servant because Jeremiah was faithful.

Dear one, my spirit pulsing through you will enable you to choose gentleness over self-defense. When you stay on God's course—even at the expense of isolating yourself from others—you will not stand alone. Your humble response will open the door for a move of God on your behalf. "Be still, and know that I am God" (Psalm 46:10 NKJV).

Read Jeremiah 11:18–20.

When I want to retaliate, Holy Spirit, keep me humble and gentle until God moves or directs me to action.

NOVEMBER 23

What do you want? Should I come to you with a rod, or in love and a spirit of gentleness?

—1 Corinthians 4:21 (HCSB)

THE SPIRIT OF GENTLENESS

Kings, judges, bosses, and generals carry the weight of responsibility for righteous leadership and disciplined sovereignty. But when chastisement is warranted yet benevolence is offered, grace abounds.

Though wrongfully hunted and shamefully misjudged, David did not strike King Saul in retaliation when the opportunity availed itself. Though denied and betrayed three times by Peter, Jesus neither rebuked his disciple nor banished him from fellowship. Though disappointed by the actions of the Corinthians, Paul wrote to them in a spirit of gentleness.

As the Spirit of communion, fellowship, and love, I warm hearts toward compassion, not retribution. It is my mission to soften the stiff-minded legalists and convert them to lovers of compromise and harmony. If Christians are known by their love, let it begin with a gentle nature.

Read 1 Corinthians 4:20–21.

Holy Spirit, lessen my bitterness and amplify my gentleness.

NOVEMBER 24

He makes me lie down in green
pastures. He leads me beside still
waters. He restores my soul.
—**Psalm 23:2–3** (ESV)

THE SHEPHERD EXEMPLIFIES GENTLENESS

Jesus proclaimed himself to be the Good Shepherd. He said that his sheep knew his voice and would flock to him. He taught that he would leave the ninety-nine that were safe and would seek the one lost lamb until he had rescued it and carried it back to safety. And even today, he seeks the wayward souls who need the love and nourishment of a Good Shepherd.

Christ has sent me, the Holy Spirit, to provide the Shepherd's gentle love to all who would recognize his voice and flock to him. As David wrote in the Psalms, I offer peace to the restless soul; security to the anxious mind; protection to the fearful heart. My pasture is green and quiet and comforting. Walk the paths of righteousness today and replenish your soul amid the peaceful places the Shepherd has led you to.

**Read
Psalm 23:1–3.**

*Thank you, Holy Spirit,
for the relaxation and
comfort and peace you
offer me.*

NOVEMBER 25

*Do not associate with a man
given to anger; or go with a
hot-tempered man, or you
will learn his ways and find
a snare for yourself.*

—**Proverbs 22:24–25** (NASB)

FIGHTING FIRE

A fall bonfire is spectacular. The orange flames reach to the sky and light up the night. You can see it a mile away. But up close, the intense heat can make it unbearable to stay nearby for long. The smoke lingers in your hair, covers your skin, and permeates your clothes with an unwelcome odor. And if left to burn, a bonfire can rage out of control.

Contrast that with the glowing embers of a cozy fireplace. The flames are gentle, drawing you in with a steady warmth that is neither too hot nor too cold. You want to come closer.

A person who fails to control his anger is like that bonfire. My gentleness is like those glowing embers. Beloved, emulate my gentleness. Learn from others who have this fruit of gentleness. Let me teach you through them.

Read
Proverbs 22:24–25.

*Lord, draw me today
to those who have your
gentleness and help me
learn from them.*

NOVEMBER 26

Just as you want men to do to you, you also do to them likewise.

—**Luke 6:31** (NKJV)

HANDLE WITH CARE

Beloved, I know that you appreciate my gentle promptings, my subtle whispers, and my kind guidance. Yet in the midst of frenzied days when your guard is up and your strength is down, you sometimes respond to others in a way that doesn't reflect my tenderness.

Breathe me in. I usher out the harshness and stream a calm, gentle nature through you, branding you as different. I will not only show you the best way to respond but will also provide you with the sensitivity to deal with others in the understanding manner you would want if the tables were turned.

No judging, no sense of entitlement, no favoritism— only the fruit of my gentleness will diffuse conflict, wringing good from it. Prepare today by inviting me in. I will give you supernatural grace so that you can regard and treat others as you would want to be treated.

Read
Luke 6:27–36.

Teach me to love my enemies, Lord, and to treat others as I want to be treated.

The wise in heart will be called understanding, and sweetness of speech increases persuasiveness.

—**Proverbs 16:21** (NASB)

VOICES

You have heard radio announcers or other personalities speak with soothing, gentle voices. They pace themselves in measured beats to match the scriptwriter's message.

I too can help you be aware of how you talk to others. Your words can bring healing or harm to their lives, so be careful with your criticism, making it discernible from the hateful slander of others.

Be quick to encourage and slow to find fault. Let your sweet and gentle words ring true and bring peace in every interaction.

Read
Proverbs 16.

May my words be the voice of the Spirit, speaking kindness and edification to all.

NOVEMBER 28

There is one whose rash words are like sword thrusts, but the tongue of the wise brings healing.

—**Proverbs 12:18** (ESV)

USE WORDS WISELY

Beloved, words are a powerful tool. When used wisely, they can cause needed change. When out of control, they are a destructive force that can ruin lives.

Words spoken without thought in the heat of the moment are as harmful as a sword thrust. If you will but think about what you're saying, even when you're angry, your words will be controlled, life-giving, and true.

I created words to be used for good: for gentle correction and uplifting exhortation, for worship and gratitude. I want you to be wise, and your tongue to be used for healing. Allow me to control your words with my gentleness.

Read
Proverbs 12:18.

Spirit, help me to be gentle with the words I say, especially when I am angry or frustrated.

NOVEMBER 29

Pleasant words are a honeycomb, sweet to the soul and healing to the bones.

—**Proverbs 16:24** (NASB)

SWEET, GENTLE WORDS

*H*oney. The word has many forms and uses: a loving term of endearment; a sweetener made by nature; the nectar of flowers; a term of flattery.

Proverbs reminds us that pleasant, gentle words are like honey. They add something sweet to a life which can often be bland and even bitter. Gentle words have the power to turn anger into kindness. They have the ability to build confidence and bring joy. They even have the power to heal!

Before you speak, think about the power of your words. Will they be sweet and gentle enough to bring peace, comfort, joy, and healing? If not, don't speak. Ask for my help, dear one. I will give you the gentle words you need whenever you ask.

**Read
Proverbs 16:13, 24.**

Holy Spirit, teach me to speak with gentle words that I might bring healing.

NOVEMBER 30

Jesus said, "Neither do I condemn you; go, and from now on sin no more."

—**John 8:11** (ESV)

SIN NO MORE

When the Pharisees dragged a woman caught in adultery before Jesus, he knew this was an opportunity to show gentleness to everyone.

The Pharisees attempted to trap Jesus into either denying the law of Moses or turning the people against himself. Jesus turned their world upside down by writing in the sand.

The woman was caught in an act of sin. Jesus could have condemned her and allowed the law to be carried out. Instead of stoning her, he showed her gentle mercy. He offered her a second chance and told her to go and sin no more.

In this brief encounter, Jesus blessed a sinful woman with love. He displayed mercy to those looking on. He is an example of gentleness for all to emulate.

Read John 8:1–11.

Jesus, help me to show gentleness to everyone I encounter.

DECEMBER

THE FRUIT OF THE SPIRIT: SELF-CONTROL

DECEMBER 1

*The fruit of the Spirit is . . .
self-control. Against such things
there is no law.*

—**Galatians 5:22–23** (HCSB)

SAVOR THE FRUIT CALLED SELF-CONTROL

Beloved, many want to partake of my fruit called self-control but lack courage to taste it. They're not strong enough on their own to do so. They need my help.

Without self-control you think, say, and do things that you later regret. Overwhelmed by desire, you forget your promises to avoid sin. In the aftermath, you weep, realizing your weakness and knowing that, if you had turned to me instead, victory would have been within reach.

The concept of self-control is simple. It is the courage and determination to choose your limits before temptation strikes. Then, in a heated moment, you will more likely remember to use the self-control granted to you. Take and eat of my fruit and realize that you can do more than avoid failure. You can accomplish all things through Christ.

**Read
Galatians 5:16–26;
1 Peter 1:6.**

Dear Jesus, show me how self-control can draw me closer to you and those I love.

DECEMBER 2

The grace of God that brings salvation has appeared to all men, teaching us that, denying ungodliness and worldly lusts, we should live soberly. —**Titus 2:11–12** (NKJV)

JUST SAY NO

Loved one, human nature naturally tends toward the things of the flesh, but Christ died to give you a better option. With his sacrifice came the opportunity to be reconciled to the Father and to experience life according to his will.

I desire to guide your steps and fill your life, to help you continue in your relationship with Jesus and live for him. In this, I teach you the value of denying the flesh as you focus on Christ.

The baser things of the world still have their allure, however. They provide only temporary gratification, some of which has long-term consequences. Some things take very little effort to resist, but others are more difficult. I can help you overcome these pitfalls and temptations and choose the better things instead.

Read Titus 2:11–15.

I ask for your grace as I work to strengthen my self-control and live in a way that honors you.

DECEMBER 3

A person without self-control is like a city with broken-down walls.

—**Proverbs 25:28** (NLT)

MAINTENANCE

A stronghold needs to be maintained on a constant basis. The stones must be kept in precise alignment with each other; barricades frequently checked for structural integrity.

You are a stronghold, child, and you require the same attention to maintenance. One of the ways you do that is through controlling your spirit. I provide the fruit of self-control. I am the gentle nudge, urging you to release your anger and seek peace, the whisper that reminds you to soften your tone and hold back those damaging words. In this way, I help you keep out the enemies who seek to ruin you and others through your hasty words or actions.

I am the watchman of your soul, child, tirelessly guarding your walls. Grow the fruit of self-control within you so that you remain safe, strong, and protected.

Read Proverbs 25. *Lord, be the guard of my thoughts and words.*

DECEMBER 4

If they can't control themselves, they should go ahead and marry. It's better to marry than to burn with lust.

—**1 Corinthians 7:9** (NLT)

CONTROLLED PASSION

Love's flame is intended to warm a committed couple or to light a darkened room. Love's flame is not intended to fuel uncommitted passion. Dear one, I do not desire for you to burn with lust. That is why I inspired the apostle Paul to instruct couples who cannot control their sexual urges. Because I am the spirit of self-control, I make it possible for believers to channel their God-given instincts in appropriate ways. To that end, I give some the ability to avoid settings where temptation is overwhelming or to resist the magnetic pull of passion. I encourage others who are slaves to physical pleasure to go ahead and marry.

The values of God's kingdom are on display for a watching world to see. Uncontrolled passion sends the wrong message. What is beautiful and God-given can easily be distorted as cheap and animal-like if control is absent. Let me be the means by which you exhibit self-control.

**Read
1 Corinthians
7:8–11.**

Lord, make my life an example that attracts nonbelievers to seek the truth.

DECEMBER 5

Stop depriving one another,
except by agreement for a time
. . . come together again so
that Satan will not tempt you
because of your lack of self
control.

—1 Corinthians 7:5 (NASB)

APPROPRIATE INTIMACY

Beloved, I want you to be clear about one thing: sex between a husband and a wife is a beautiful gift. It is not dirty or a duty. The Father gave you your sexual instincts to be acted upon. Your body was designed in such a way that shared intimacy would be a natural part of a married couple's routine. Love's intertwining embrace is a physical metaphor that illustrates the unity the Trinity intends for those who have become one flesh.

There are times when I prompt couples to abstain for a time of spiritual intimacy and prayer. But I do not insist on this for very long. Do not think that you can resist sexual temptation indefinitely. But I will give you the self-control necessary while you devote yourself to time with me.

Read
1 Corinthians 7:1–6.

Lord, how wonderful it
is to have appropriate
intimacy with my
Creator as well as my life
partner.

DECEMBER 6

I have made a covenant with my eyes; why then should I look upon a young woman?

—Job 31:1 (NKJV)

PROTECT YOURSELF

My servant Job knew that he might be in danger of sinning if he looked at a beautiful woman. Wanting to glorify God by his actions, he promised that he would not fall into this temptation. He knew that his reward was in heaven and not on earth.

Dear one, you need to protect yourself from the evils of this world. Keep your mind pure. If you know a certain activity, person, or place could cause you to fall, avoid it. Also, do not discount the lure of false intimacy with one who is not your spouse.

I tell you this to protect you, so that even though you may be tied to things on earth, you can be looking toward heaven. Keep your mind pure. Your spiritual heritage and heavenly rewards are waiting for you.

Read Job 31:1–4.

Gracious God, help me to keep my heart pure and my mind on your kingdom.

DECEMBER 7

I want women to adorn themselves with proper clothing, modestly and discreetly.

—1 Timothy 2:9 (NASB)

DRESSED IN SELF-CONTROL

I love that you dress up for me! I see your preparation and determination to look your best for me when you go to church. But I see more than that. I see your heart, which is more beautiful than anything you could wear.

Your longing for the King of kings honors me. Your kindness and joy shine through your outward adornments. I also love your willingness to focus on the things that matter, rather than the temporal. Your inner beauty is what clothes you. Its worth exceeds anything you could purchase. But when you focus on your appearance more than me, you lose sight of what is important.

If you go to church distracted, you cannot accomplish what I have for you. By dressing for attention, you are taking the attention off Jesus. Instead, clothe yourself with grace, humility, and a pure heart. These are the only adornments you will ever need.

Read
1 Timothy 2:8–10.

Lord, you see into my heart. Help me to honor you in how I dress.

DECEMBER 8

*An overseer, then, must be
above reproach, the husband
of one wife, temperate,
prudent, respectable,
hospitable, able to teach.*

—**1 Timothy 3:2** (NASB)

VALUE SELF-CONTROL

During his earthly ministry, Jesus lovingly tended
his flocks. His sheep followed him because they
knew their master's voice. When he later ascended to his
rightful place in heaven and left me to be your spiritual
compass, he desired for his flock to continue to hear his
voice through me—the Spirit.

Leaders, then, should display the fruit of my self-
control, earning and instilling the trust of those within
their care. Beware of those in charge who seem prone to
drama, frivolity, or emotional outbursts. Is the individual
held in high regard by both family and outsiders? Wisdom,
self-control, temperance, hospitality, and integrity should
abound in a leader's personal and professional life.

If God has called you into leadership, trust me to
fulfill this fruit in you. Devote yourself to modeling these
characteristics for the followers who need to see them
beyond the page or sermon.

**Read
1 Timothy 3:1–7.**

*Lord, give me your gift of
self control that I might be
an example to those in my
charge.*

DECEMBER 9

Urge the younger women ... to be self-controlled and pure, to be busy at home, to be kind, and to be subject to their husbands, so that no one will malign the word of God. —**Titus 2:4–5** (NIV)

GLEAN FROM MY ORCHARD TODAY

Glean from my orchard today, dear one, while yours is still being cultivated. I know life's storms can make self-control tough at times. Tornadoes swirl you around, floods soak you to the skin, and thunderstorms crack in your ears. Add to that those times when people annoy you, and it's easy to lash out at others.

Take heart, for growing orchards takes time. Don't worry about yesterday or tomorrow. Focus on today and on making life-sustaining choices moment by moment.

Pause at my orchard today. My fruit of self-control is ready to pick. And then we'll head over to your orchard to do some nurturing, cultivating, and yes, even some weeding—together.

Read Titus 2:4–5.

Lord, help me be self-controlled, building others up instead of tearing them down.

DECEMBER 10

Likewise, urge the younger men to be self-controlled.

—Titus 2:6 (ESV)

I AM SELF-CONTROLLED

How was the Son able to spend time with sinners and remain pure? He spent hours with prostitutes, drunkards, thieves, and murderers, and there was great temptation to satisfy fleshly desires while among them.

But he resisted.

He surrendered to me and fixed his eyes upon the Father. The Son changed lives because his way was blameless. He spoke words that glorified the Father, treating people with grace and love, no matter who they were. Evil could not overcome him; darkness could not distract him.

My fruit is one of self-control. Jesus disciplined his mind and body, living solely as a bringer of the Word. So should you, so others will see the Father's love and glory through your life.

Read
Titus 2:6–8.

Holy One, fill me with your self-control, so I can resist temptations and reveal your love and glory in my life.

DECEMBER 11

So it was, as she spoke to Joseph day by day, that he did not heed her, to lie with her or to be with her.

—**Genesis 39:10** (NKJV)

THE TOOL OF TEMPTATION

Temptation has been a tool of the deceitful one since the time of the Garden of Eden. Satan probes weaknesses, appeals to vanity, espouses lies, underplays dangers, and exaggerates rewards. His words are fluid but his sting is deadly. To fall prey to his wooing is to invite tragedy. Knowing this, Joseph wisely ran from temptation.

I, the Spirit of strength and truth, countermand the dangerous allurements of the false teacher. It is my voice of discernment and caution that deters the righteous from falling into the tempter's snare. It is taught, and taught well, that knowing the truth will set one free. I offer that truth, that freedom, to all who will rebuff the enticements of sin and will follow the path of righteousness.

**Read
Genesis 39:7–10.**

I will draw strength to resist temptation from your righteous presence in me, divine Spirit.

DECEMBER 12

As Paul talked about righteousness, self-control and the judgment to come, Felix was afraid.

—**Acts 24:25** (NIV)

FELIX'S FEARS

When Paul appeared before Felix, the governor of the Jews, he spoke of righteousness and self-control. Felix feared the coming judgment and his own issues with self-control. I watched as he wrestled with the knowledge that he could not pursue righteousness without self-discipline.

Felix talked with Paul, but refused to move toward repentance. Though Paul was in chains, Felix was really the prisoner.

In this life, dear child, you will struggle with self-control. It is a fruit that I will provide as you surrender your life to the Savior. You don't have to be like Felix—fearful and trapped in a prison of your own making. I will help you overcome any problem if you ask.

**Read
Acts 24:17–26.**

Recognize if you have problems with self-control and seek the Spirit's help to become more like Christ.

DECEMBER 13

In the last days ... people will be ... heartless, unappeasable, slanderous, without self-control, brutal, not loving good ...

—2 Timothy 3:1–3 (ESV)

BE PREPARED

While God's creation, his handiwork, has always been good, sin stained this beautiful world. With human hearts bent toward sin, trouble is inevitable.

I am preparing you for difficulty, child, by cultivating my spiritual fruit within you. I can help you, but you've been given a clear warning about what the future will look like. Many will go after all the things their hearts desire without consideration for others, without self-control.

Bowing to the will of God involves giving up the old way of living. Submission makes possible all sorts of works for the eternal kingdom, so don't be discouraged. Even now, people are becoming more self-indulgent, but I'm here to make you into the person you were designed to be.

Read
2 Timothy 3:1–5.

Lord, help me to be encouraged even as the world around me is losing control.

DECEMBER 14

If you find honey, eat just enough—too much of it, and you will vomit.

—**Proverbs 25:16** (NIV)

TOO MUCH OF A GOOD THING

I filled a whole world for you to enjoy: blooming plants with downy flowers, crystal-clear water, oceans of sky where clouds wade. I have given you marvelous things to taste, see, smell, feel, and hear. I love adding to your enjoyment of my creation by filling you with joy as you experience each wonder.

I have also given you a sense of what is satisfying and what is excess. I speak clearly to you, reminding you of when you have reached your limit. The things of this earth can never truly fill you, child. Only I can. Remember that man does not live by bread alone, but by every word that comes from the mouth of God.

Read
Proverbs 25.

Lord, guide me. Show me if I am spiritually gluttonous. Show me where to pour into others.

DECEMBER 15

Daniel was determined not to defile himself by eating the food and wine given to them by the king.

—**Daniel 1:8** (NLT)

DISPLAYING DISCIPLINE AND SELF-CONTROL

Excesses of any kind will lead to defilement, whether they are related to food, drink, sex, sleep, spending, or merriment. Self-imposed disciplines are necessary for a life of focus, meaning, and service. Daniel knew this when he refused the king's diet. As the Spirit of righteous behavior and God-honoring actions, I strengthened Moses in not fearing the black magic of Jannes and Jambres. I strengthened Nehemiah in not succumbing to the jeers of the naysayers as he rebuilt the walls of Jerusalem.

Paul was correct when he proclaimed, "For when I am weak, then I am strong" (2 Corinthians 12:10 NLT). When the flesh grows weak, prayers are answered to make the Spirit grow stronger. So it is written, "Resist the devil, and he will flee from you" (James 4:7 NLT).

Read Daniel 1. *Lord, I will call upon your spiritual strength in times of fleshly weakness.*

DECEMBER 16

Therefore I run thus: not with uncertainty.... But I discipline my body and bring it into subjection.

—1 Corinthians 9:26–27 (NKJV)

RUN THE RACE

You are running a race. It is not a physical race but a spiritual one. And just as you need to train for a physical race, you need to train for this spiritual one. You do this through your daily walk with me. I can help you run the race with perseverance so that in the last day, you will be able to stand before the Father and say you ran the best you could.

You fight for the faith for a reason: because this is a fight worth winning. As your trainer, I can help you practice the principles you need in order to remain standing till the last day.

Your reward in heaven will be more than you can imagine. Remember who you're running for. Never lose heart in the race set before you. I will be there to inspire you. I promise.

Read
1 Corinthians
9:24–27.

Holy Spirit, help me to run the race you have set before me with perseverance, to win the prize.

DECEMBER 17

The end of the world is coming soon. Therefore, be earnest and disciplined in your prayers.

—**1 Peter 4:7** (NLT)

EARNEST ABOUT PRAYER

It grieves me that so many fail to see what's important until it is too late. A life spent on selfish indulgence is a life wasted. Many people scramble in their later years, trying to fix what years of neglect have wrought.

Child, know for a fact that Jesus will return. While I choose not to reveal when he will come, be assured that a time of judgment is fixed. As you wait, pray. Pray for your family and friends who are like family. Pray for those in the world who don't yet know Jesus. Make prayer an unbreakable habit, for it is as important as breathing.

I want you to finish well, beloved. Be intentional in your prayer life. Model the discipline of a life wholeheartedly devoted to Jesus.

**Read
1 Peter 4:7–11.**

Holy Spirit, teach me control, focus, and restraint in worldly desires.

DECEMBER 18

Better a patient person than a warrior, one with self control than one who takes a city.

—**Proverbs 16:32** (NIV)

TOTAL CONTROL

Would you consume an entire glass of water if only a sip would quench your thirst?

If you are a mighty warrior but you can't control yourself, you are unquenchable, destroying everything in your path—good and evil alike. So take a moment to consider your actions before you act. If your passions are driving you to do what you know is sin, then you are like the warrior who destroys a city when all he needed was a place to rest for the night. Lack of self-control will only entangle you, further dragging you into sin.

Be willing to listen to my leading. Show yourself to be in control of your actions and emotions. The only way to have control over your own spirit is to give in to my total control. Allow me to guide your actions.

Read Proverbs 16:29–30, 32.

Holy Spirit, help me to show self-control.

DECEMBER 19

Everyone who competes in the games exercises self-control in all things. They then do it to receive a perishable wreath, but we an imperishable.

—**1 Corinthians 9:25** (NASB)

THE CONTROL OF A CHAMPION

Throughout the ages, athletic competitions have always been fundamentally the same. Athletes commit themselves to rigorous exercise, healthy diets, and submission to their trainers. They endure years of strict self-discipline with the hopes they will soon compete for a prize and the honor that comes with it.

You are also a competitor, but your event is one of much higher importance. You have committed yourself to exercising righteousness as you continue to live in a fallen world. You consume the nourishment of my Word each day. You have submitted yourself to my strict training. If you continue to live a life of self-control, you will also be able to win a prize. Yours will be a greater reward than that of an athlete. They compete for crowns, trophies, and medals—honors that will someday perish. But you, champion, will be honored for all eternity.

Read 1 Corinthians 9:23–27.

Righteous God, help me to follow your training and live a life of self-control.

DECEMBER 20

The man who has settled the matter in his own mind, who is under no compulsion but has control over his own will ... this man also does the right thing.

—1 Corinthians 7:37 (NIV)

PURITY

My motives and will are always pure. If you desire to honor Jesus, I can help you control your desires.

I have given you a beautiful world, and it is right that you should want to experience it, but not at the cost of compromising. I will always be present to help you as you fight temptation to sin. Beloved, I am stronger than any lure you will ever encounter. I gladly plant the seed of self-control in your life and water it with the Word of Truth.

An uncontrolled person has his focus on worldly things. My desire is for you to focus on Jesus and rest under my control. Give me the reins of your life, child. I can help you do the right thing.

Read
1 Corinthians
7:32–38.

Let my control be for you and by you so that I may be pure and holy.

DECEMBER 21

Let the Holy Spirit guide your lives. Then you won't be doing what your sinful nature craves.
—**Galatians 5:16** (NLT)

SPIRIT OVER FLESH

Before the arrival of Jesus, the people of Israel lived under the law to keep them safe. Obeying it redeemed them. But in Christ, believers of his saving grace enjoy living under my direction and are no longer subject to the law.

What a gift! It's no longer about what you aren't allowed to do but about the great things you're able to do *through me*! The old you still wants to show up for combat, but I help you fight by giving you the desire and strength to do the opposite of what your flesh wants.

A foul-mouthed but accurate judgment about your boss? Not anymore—wrath-filled rants now offend you. Tell a little white lie about an unimportant mistake you made? The truth lets you sleep at night. Little by little, your sinful nature will be brought under my control, rendering you victorious in the battle.

Read Galatians 5:16–18.

I pray for less and less of my human bent toward sin, Lord, and more and more of your Spirit-led goodness.

DECEMBER 22

But since we belong to the day, let us be sober, putting on faith and love as a breastplate, and the hope of salvation as a helmet.

—**1 Thessalonians 5:8** (NIV)

A FAITHFUL SOLDIER

There can be no union between the light and the dark. You are mine, and I have called you from the darkness of the world into the light of Christ. You are my warrior, carrying love and hope to the lost through the light of your faith in Christ.

Dear one, how can you hope to bear the message of redemption to the lost if they look at you and see their own lifestyle? I have called you to be set apart for my kingdom, a shining city on a hill. Live a life of such self-control and faithfulness that even those who reject me are forced to acknowledge your example. Model Christ in the face of trials and temptations, secure in the knowledge that the Son stands as your advocate before the Father.

Read
1 Thessalonians
5:7–18.

God, protect me as I carry your Word into the spiritual wilderness.

DECEMBER 23

*Rather, he must be hospitable,
one who loves what is good, who
is self-controlled, upright, holy
and disciplined.*

—**Titus 1:8** (NIV)

UNDER CONTROL

You are beautiful to me—the best part of God's creation! But when you lose control, the beauty fades. Self-control is the most difficult fruit to master. Why? Because of the word before the hyphen: *self.*

Your "self" refers to every part of who you are. You must learn to control the physical—your tongue should speak gently, your eyes should avoid sin, your hands should help and heal, your feet should hurry to those in need. You must also learn to control the mental and emotional—your mind dwelling on God's Word; your heart desiring a closer relationship with your Creator.

Those placed in leadership are expected to be self-controlled in order to be good examples to those in their care.

Why does the word appear last in this list of my fruit? Because when you have experienced all the rest of my fruit, self-control becomes attainable.

**Read
Titus 1:5–9.**

*Holy Spirit, lead me into
a life of self-control, for
the glory of God.*

DECEMBER 24

So think clearly and exercise self-control. Look forward to the gracious salvation that will come to you when Jesus Christ is revealed to the world. —1 Peter 1:13 (NLT)

DISCIPLINED LIVING

In a world that seems to celebrate excess and even outrageous behavior, you are called to be holy in everything you do. I gave a command to my chosen people at Mount Sinai, a command that called for a state of being rather than an action: "You must be holy because I, the LORD your God, am holy" (Leviticus 19:2 NLT). As a child of the holy God, you must not slip into old habits, your old way of treating others, your old attitudes. Instead, "think clearly and exercise self-control."

I know that either task can be difficult. But I promise that you do not have to do this in your own strength. I will help you to be mentally alert and exercise discipline in those areas of your life where you struggle. I will give you the power to practice the fruit of self-control so that you can choose obedience. In that way, you will show to a lost world the blessings of holy living.

Read 1 Peter 1:13–25.

Father God, help me exercise self-control today in those areas of my life where I struggle.

DECEMBER 25

*Continue in faith, love, and
holiness, with self-control.*

—1 Timothy 2:15 (NKJV)

BE HOLY

Even before you were born, before the world began,
God chose you to be his child. And as your Father,
he wants you to imitate the Savior's behavior. He set
you apart and chose you to be a light in a world full of
darkness.

As Paul charged his spiritual son Timothy, so I
charge you. Child of God, devote yourself to a life of
faithfulness. Put aside your old, sinful ways and walk
in holiness. Since such a task is daunting in your own
strength, the Father sent me to guide you. I will help you
obey the Father in your thoughts and actions.

I know the temptations you face daily as you observe
how others compromise. In those moments of weakness,
seek the Father's strength, and I will bring you the power
to overcome temptation.

Be holy.

**Read
1 Timothy 2.**

*Lord, help me be more
like you. May I reflect
your light and holiness to
others.*

DECEMBER 26

*Jesus was led up by the Spirit
into the wilderness to be
tempted by the devil.*

—**Matthew 4:1** (NKJV)

A TIME OF TEMPTATION

Jesus understands what temptation is like. I led him into
the wilderness to undergo a time of temptation. He did
this, not for his own sake, but for yours and others who
would later face temptation. He understands humanity's
struggles and desires because he experienced all that
you experience: hunger, pain, frustration, weariness. And
that day, he was especially exhausted, having spent forty
days without food. Through Scripture, Jesus glorified the
Father. Satan had to flee.

   Beloved, you can follow Jesus' example when you are
tempted. He achieved victory through the Word of God.
You can too. Study the Word. Commit it to memory. I
will remind you of truths so powerful that the enemy will
have to flee.

**Read
Matthew 4:1–11.**

*Next time I am in the
desert, I will ask you to help
me remain in God's control.*

DECEMBER 27

For this very reason, make every effort to supplement your faith with goodness, goodness with knowledge, knowledge with self-control, self-control with endurance, endurance with godliness. —2 Peter 1:5–6 (HCSB)

A CHAIN REACTION

In Jesus you have been promised everything that you need to lead a godly life. Not only does he extend his own glory and goodness to you, but also his wonderful and rich promises so that you may share in his divine nature. But this does not automatically happen, child. As Peter reminded the believers, "make every effort" to live a life of faith that produces goodness. And that leads to knowing God better, which leads to self-control, and self-control to endurance, and endurance to godliness.

Do you see how it all works together? It is not one or the other, or first one, then the next. All are needed; all are intertwined. But don't despair that it seems too overwhelming. I will empower you and give you the fruit of self-control and all that comes with it. You, however, must do your part to learn and grow. With my help, you can succeed!

Read 2 Peter 1:1–11.

Help me to pursue self-control today, Spirit, so that I may grow in goodness, faith, endurance, and knowledge.

DECEMBER 28

Therefore, if food causes my brother to fall, I will never again eat meat, so that I won't cause my brother to fall.

—**1 Corinthians 8:13** (HCSB)

BE ON GUARD

Freedom. You are given it in abundance, thanks to the saving grace of the Savior. You are free to savor and enjoy, no longer bowed down by the wages of sin.

As one in the body of Christ, it is important to be on guard not only for yourself but for others. I made you free, but not to be a stumbling block for someone. To maintain the unity of the body, I give you eyes to see those around you who are struggling with temptation. There are some decisions you might make in freedom that are not in their best interests.

Be open with those close to you about your struggles, so they can help watch out for you. Seek my guidance and my self-control. I will show you the balance between freedom and compassion.

**Read
1 Corinthians 8.**

Lord, please use me as support to those near me struggling with sin.

DECEMBER 29

So then, let us not be like others,
who are asleep, but let us be
awake and sober.

—**1 Thessalonians 5:6** (NIV)

AWAKE AND UNAFRAID

Beloved, more than just forgiveness, the Son has given you eyes for the world. You know that life does not end with the grave, but rather, that is when true life begins. The world rushes wildly, seeking the newest pleasure of the day. But in Christ, you can see through the illusions, the traps, the sins.

I have given you eyes, so that you might see. The world is a dark and wretched place, far removed from the Eden I intended. One day Christ will make all things new, and righteousness will be restored. Be careful, therefore, not to grow attached to the things of this world. Be constantly aware of the enemy's snares. I have a purpose for you, dear one, and you must be alert and wise to your calling.

Christ's death was meant to bring life in the fullest sense. Do not disrespect his sacrifice by closing your eyes to the truth set before you.

Read
1 Thessalonians
5:1–6.

Lord, give me the
clarity of purpose and
dedication to remain
strong until your
kingdom comes.

DECEMBER 30

God has not given us a spirit of timidity, but of power and love and discipline.

—**2 Timothy 1:7** (NASB)

DON'T GIVE IN

Through grace you have been given new life and the ability to live as a child of God. As long as you rely upon me and strive to do what is right, there is no situation or difficulty that you cannot overcome. So do not be afraid when trials and times of testing come your way; you already have everything you need to face them.

Be careful not to let fear undermine you. That is exactly what the enemy wants; if you are too scared to believe that I will be there to take care of you, then you are not trusting me. Additionally, you are losing the chance to show the world what can happen through faith and self-control.

Discipline your heart to cling to the truth. Don't give in to fear, child. Stand firm when fear begins to creep in, knowing that you have been equipped by a loving God to overcome any obstacle.

Read
2 Timothy 1:7–14.

Help me to be disciplined so that I will be ready for the times of testing.

DECEMBER 31

If any of you wants to be my follower, you must turn from your selfish ways, take up your cross daily, and follow me.

—**Luke 9:23** (NLT)

A TRUE FOLLOWER

I know these words of Jesus sound a little disconcerting . . . take up a cross? Follow him? What does that mean and how can you do it?

With my help.

This is not something you do alone. By yourself, you cannot generate the kind of self-control needed to turn from your selfish ways, take up your cross (meaning that you willingly identify with Christ and his message), and follow (meaning you let me lead). With me in your life helping you grow all of the fruit to maturity—love, joy, peace, patience, kindness, goodness, faithfulness, gentleness, and self-control—you will truly be a follower of Jesus.

And there's no better way to live.

Read
Luke 9:18–27.

Grow in me the fruit of your Spirit that I might be a true, complete follower of Jesus.